Hal Leonard Student Piano Library

Teacher's Guide

Piano Lessons Book 2

Contents

Authors
**Barbara Kreader, Fred Kern,
Phillip Keveren, Mona Rejino**

Consultants
Tony Caramia, Bruce Berr,
Richard Rejino

*Director,
Educational Keyboard Publications*
Margaret Otwell

Editor
Janet Medley

Illustrator
Fred Bell

ISBN 0-634-05590-9

HAL•LEONARD®
CORPORATION

7777 W. BLUEMOUND RD. P.O. BOX 13819 MILWAUKEE, WI 53213

In Australia Contact:
Hal Leonard Australia Pty. Ltd.
22 Taunton Drive P.O. Box 5130
Cheltenham East, 3192 Victoria, Australia
Email: ausadmin@halleonard.com

Visit Hal Leonard Online at
www.halleonard.com

The Hal Leonard Student Piano Library

When music excites our interest and imagination, we eagerly put our hearts into learning it. The music in the **Hal Leonard Student Piano Library** encourages practice, progress, confidence, and best of all – success! Students respond with enthusiasm to the:

- variety of styles and moods
- natural rhythmic flow, singable melodies and lyrics
- exceptional teacher accompaniments
- improvisations threaded throughout the series
- Instrumental Accompaniments for every piece available on CD or General MIDI disk.

When new concepts have an immediate application to the music, the effort it takes to learn these skills seems worth it. Teachers appreciate the:

- realistic pacing that challenges without overwhelming
- clear and concise presentation of concepts
- uncluttered page lay-out that keeps the focus on the music.

The Library is available in five levels. Each level includes a Lesson Book and several supplementary books:

PIANO PRACTICE GAMES

Imaginative preparation activities to introduce pieces in the Piano Lessons books.

PIANO THEORY WORKBOOK

Fun and creative assignments that introduce the language of music and its symbols.

PIANO SOLOS

Original performance repertoire featuring 14 different composers. Available with instrumental accompaniments on CD or General MIDI disk.

PIANO TECHNIQUE

Etudes to develop physical mastery of the keyboard with optional instrumental accompaniments on CD or General MIDI disk.

NOTESPELLER FOR PIANO

By Karen Harrington
Music worksheets and games in a story-book format that enhance reading and writing skills.

FOREWORD

Method books give you the materials you need, yet only the relationship between you and the student can bring the music to life. This *Teacher's Guide* is intended to suggest possible ways to introduce and work with each piece in *Piano Lessons Book 2* of the **Hal Leonard Student Piano Library**.

New Concepts: highlight the new musical ideas presented in each piece

Touch & Sound: highlight the physical skills needed to create the appropriate sound and mood of each piece

Review: highlights those concepts that may need continued work

The teaching suggestions are divided into the following categories:

Prepare	Practice	Perform
Introduces the coordination and rhythm of each piece before combining those aspects of the music with pitch reading.	Includes steps to learning each piece, such as blocking, comparing phrases, and saying note names or intervals out loud.	Includes suggestions for putting all the steps together to play each piece accurately and in the appropriate tempo, mood, and style.

Many activities throughout this book include accompaniments that can be added in the following ways:

Teacher   Audio CD   General MIDI Disk

Each page also includes references to the coordinated activities in *Piano Practice Games*, *Piano Theory Workbook*, *Piano Technique*, *Notespeller*, *Piano Solos*, and *Music Flash Cards*.

In addition, the *Lesson Planning Charts* on pages 49-65 give you an at-a-glance view of how to coordinate all of the books and materials in Books 1-5 of the **Hal Leonard Student Piano Library**.

We hope these teaching ideas will stimulate your own unique teaching style and will help you organize your lessons in ways that keep the pleasure of making music the first priority!

Barbara Kreader   Fred Kern   Phillip Keveren   Mona Rejino

Supplementary Books:

Theory Workbook
The Grand Staff –
A Musical Map pg. 2

Piano Technique
Take Another Look pg. 5
Rope Bridge pgs. 7 & 8

Notespeller
At The Ticket Booths pg. 2
Piano Park Tokens pg. 3
The Half-Note Express pg. 4

Music Flash Cards – Set A
White #8, #9, #10
Yellow #5

	New Concepts:	Whole rest ▬	Review:	*mp*
		Bass clef C D E		Stepping up
	Touch & Sound:	Passing melody between fingers 1-5		Stepping down
		in each hand		

Prepare	Practice	Perform
Student plays C D E F G in several positions all over piano keyboard. Using keyboard guide at the top of the page, student finds new bass notes C D E in the piece *Reflection*. Ask student to find all whole rests in piece.	While listening to *Reflection*, student: 1) claps rhythm and sings lyrics. 2) writes names of starting notes in the magnifying glasses. Ask student: "How is the L.H. a reflection of the R.H.?"	Student reads and plays *Reflection* with a natural pulse on beat one of each measure.

4

My Own Song
On C D E F G

Place both hands on C D E F G. Listen and feel the pulse as your teacher plays the accompaniment below.

With your right hand, play C D E F G and then play G F E D C. Experiment by mixing the letters any way you want and make up your own song!

With your left hand, play C D E F G and then play G F E D C. Again, mix the letters any way you want and make up another song!

Have fun!

Accompaniment
Moderately (♩=120)

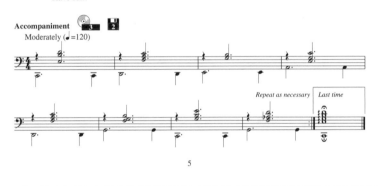

Repeat as necessary | *Last time*

5

New Concepts: Improvising in C Major position   **Review:** Bass Clef notes
C D E

Prepare	**Practice**	**Perform**
 While listening to *My Own Song On C D E F G*, student taps quarter notes, half notes and then whole notes.	Student improvises in C Major five-finger pattern in one or more positions up and down keyboard.	Encourage student to improvise freely, using one or both hands, and with one or more note values.

Supplementary Books:

Theory Workbook
*Drawing Notes
  On The Staff* pg. 3

Piano Technique
See-Saw pgs. 7 & 9

Notespeller
The Train Ride pg. 5

Ode To Joy

	Ludwig van Beethoven
	(1770 1827)
	Adapted by Fred Kern

Accompaniment (Student plays one octave higher than written.)

New Concepts:	None, review piece	**Review:**	—
			Bass C D E
Touch & Sound:	Connected tones		*f*

Prepare	**Practice**	**Perform**
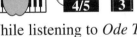 While listening to *Ode To Joy*, student points to notes and counts rhythm aloud. Ask student: "How is line two different from line one?"	Student circles all repeated notes, then points and says letter names.	Student plays and reads piece, adding more arm weight after repeat for a full, *forte* sound.

Carmen's Tune

Georges Bizet
(1838 1875)
Adapted by Fred Kern

Accompaniment (Student plays one octave higher than written.)

Lively (♩ =230)

New Concepts:	None, review piece	**Review:**	—

Touch & Sound: Playing repeated notes with thumb

Prepare	**Practice**	**Perform**
While listening to *Carmen's Tune*, student: 1) claps this rhythm:  2) plays the same rhythm with R.H. thumb on Middle C.	Student plays R.H. in a slow, deliberate manner, playing repeated notes with a bouncing motion of wrist.	Student plays *Carmen's Tune* in a brisk tempo with a natural pulse on first beat of each measure.

Supplementary Books:

Practice Games
Listen & Respond pg. 4
Read & Discover pg. 4
Imagine & Create pg. 5

Theory Workbook
Rhythm Detective pg. 6

Piano Technique
Red Light, Green Light
pgs. 11-12

Notespeller
The Canoe Ride pgs. 6-7

Piano Solos
Song Of The Orca pgs. 4-5

Music Flash Cards – Set A
Pink #14

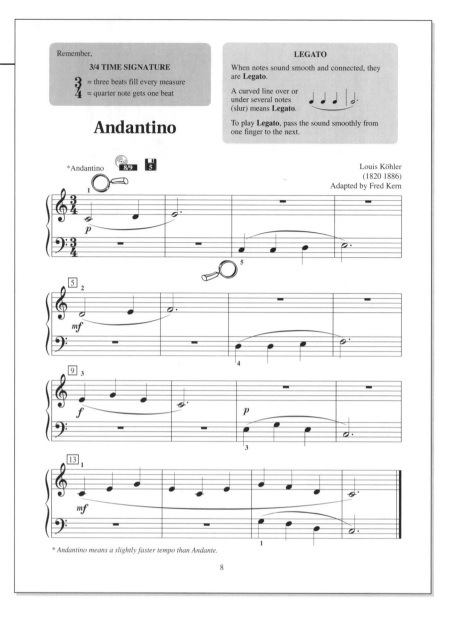

New Concepts:	Slurs, phrasing	**Review:** $\frac{3}{4}$ time signature
Touch & Sound:	*Legato* touch	

Prepare	Practice	Perform
While listening to *Andantino*, student slides index finger along slurs in book, gently lifting finger off page by raising wrist at end of each phrase.	As a warm up for m. 15-16, student plays G F E D C hands together, passing the sound smoothly from one finger to the next.	Student plays *Andantino* with a *legato* touch, gently lifting wrist at the end of each phrase.
Ask student: "How many phrases are two measures long? Four measures long?"	Student then removes the E from the above pattern and slowly plays G F D C hands together.	

Supplementary Books:

Theory Workbook
Note Name Review pg. 7

Notespeller
Name The Canoes! pg. 8

Music Flash Cards – Set A
Pink #27, #28, #29, #30
Yellow #29

New Concepts:	None, review piece	**Review:**	Tied notes
			Dynamics
Touch & Sound:	*Legato* touch		*Legato*
			3/4

Prepare	**Practice**	**Perform**

While listening to *Big Ben*, student claps and counts this rhythm:

Ask student:
"Which lines are exactly the same?" | Remind student to keep right heel on the floor when holding down the damper pedal.

This is a good review piece for **3/4** time. Make sure student holds dotted half notes for their full value. | Encourage student to experiment with piece by playing in higher and lower octaves on the keyboard.

Play song with 4 or more chimes at the end, and then ask student: "What time is it?" |

Supplementary Books:

Practice Games
Listen & Respond pg. 6
Read & Discover pg. 6

Theory Workbook
Harmonic Or Melodic? pg. 8
Harmonic 2nds And 3rds pg. 9

Piano Technique
Bee Cha-Cha pgs. 11 & 13

Notespeller
The Ferris Wheel pg. 9

New Concepts: Naming steps as 2nds
Naming skips as 3rds

Touch & Sound: Playing melodic and harmonic intervals

Review: 𝄽 , ― , ‒

Prepare	**Practice**	**Perform**

While listening to *Please, No Bees!*, student taps rhythm and sings lyrics.
 	
Ask student:
"How many harmonic 2nds are in this piece?"
  – harmonic 3rds?
  – melodic 2nds?
  – melodic 3rds?
	Student plays L.H. warm-up at top of page, then writes note names in magnifying glasses.
	
	In measure 3, instruct student to circle the melodic second between E and F. This is the only R.H. step in entire piece.
		Student reads and plays *Please, No Bees!* with a lively tempo, while the left wrist bounces lightly on the harmonic intervals.

Supplementary Books:

Practice Games
Imagine & Create pg. 7

Theory Workbook
Legato Or Staccato? pg. 10
*Drawing Legato
And Staccato Marks* pg. 11

Piano Solos
The Macaroni Cha-Cha
pgs. 6-7

Music Flash Cards – Set A
Pink #15

New Concepts:	*Staccato* symbol ♩	Review:	2nds, 3rds
			f
Touch & Sound:	Separated notes		Repeat :‖
	Staccato touch		

Prepare	Practice	Perform
While listening to *Clapping Song*, student: 1) finger-taps L.H. accompaniment on the piano cabinet. 2) plays L.H. accompaniment on the piano keyboard.	In m. 3-4, and m. 7-8, student draws a line connecting note-heads of R.H. melody. Student compares the shape of each line and then plays R.H. melody.	Student plays *Clapping Song* *staccato* with a bouncing wrist. Fingers should naturally rebound and come to rest on the piano key.

Hoedown
Janet Feldman

New Concepts:	Interval of a 4th	**Review:**	Parallel thumbs on C and D
			Staccato
Touch & Sound:	Playing both *staccato* and		*Legato*
	legato in one piece.		Melodic and harmonic intervals

Prepare	Practice	Perform
While listening to *Hoedown*, student taps and counts rhythm.	Student plays only m. 1-2 and m. 5-6, while teacher answers by playing m. 3-4 and m. 7-8.	Student plays *Hoedown* using full arm weight on the harmonic 4ths in the last measure of piece.
Ask student: "How many melodic 4ths are in this piece?" – harmonic 4ths?	Switch parts.	
Student circles all the 4ths.	Discuss the difference in touch and sound between *staccato* and *legato* sections.	

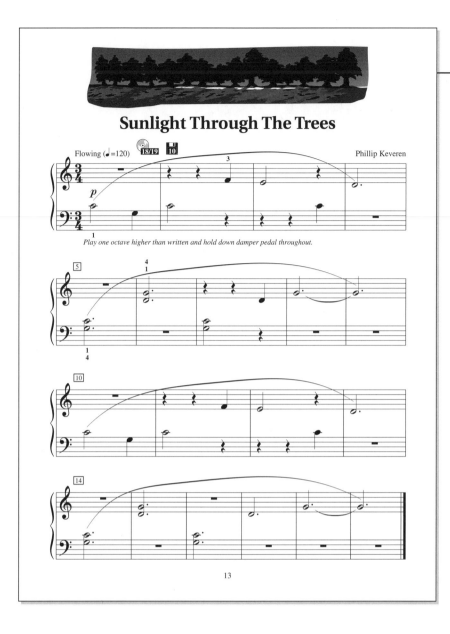

Supplementary Books:

Practice Games
Imagine & Create pgs. 10-11

Theory Workbook
Intervalasaurus pg. 13

Piano Technique
Windchimes pgs. 15 & 17

Notespeller
A Treasure Hunt pg. 11

Piano Solos
The Stream pgs. 8-9

Music Flash Cards – Set A
Yellow #30

| **New Concepts:** | Playing phrases of different lengths | **Review:** | Melodic and harmonic 4ths Tied notes |
| **Touch & Sound:** | Playing *legato* phrases with a smooth and fluid motion | | |

Prepare	**Practice**	**Perform**
 While listening to *Sunlight Through The Trees*, student: 1) claps this rhythm 2) claps and counts rhythm of piece with a natural pulse on downbeat of each measure. Ask student: "How long is each phrase?"	Since these phrases are not equal in length, make sure student holds the tied "G" notes at the end of lines 2 and 4 for their full value.	Student plays *Sunlight Through The Trees* with a soft, *legato* touch.

New Concepts:	Upbeat (pick-up note)	**Review:**	*Staccato*
			Middle C position
Touch & Sound:	Two-note harmony between hands		

Prepare	**Practice**	**Perform**

Prepare

While listening to *Bingo*, student claps rhythm and sings lyrics.

Ask student:
"How many beats are missing in the last measure?"

One count was removed from the last measure to give the beginning of the piece an upbeat (or pick-up note).

Practice

In line two, student plays the first note of each measure hands together in whole notes:

Once this is mastered, student plays line two as written.

Perform

<u>Extra for Experts</u>
Student repeats measure five 12 times while tapping foot (x) in these variations of the lyric "Bingo":

B - I - N - G - O

1) X

2) X X

3) X X X

4) X X X X

5) X X X X X

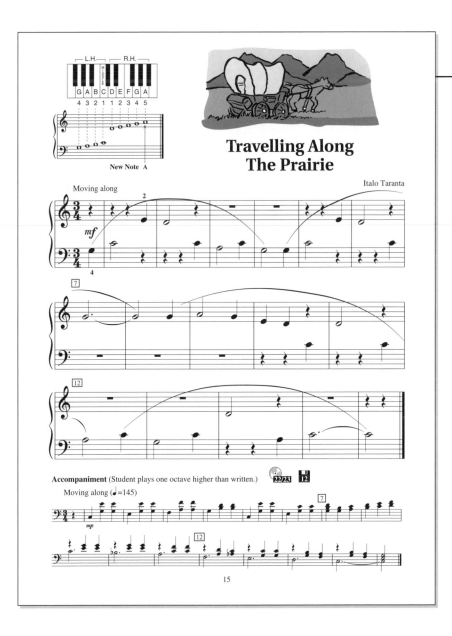

New Concepts:	Treble Clef "A"	**Review:**	Upbeat

Touch & Sound: 4-measure phrases in 3/4 time signature

Prepare	**Practice**	**Perform**
 While listening to *Travelling Along The Prairie*, student: 1) claps this rhythm  2) slides index finger along slurs, gently lifting with wrist at the end of each phrase. Ask student: "How long is each phrase?"	Ask student to compare the rhythm of each phrase. Slowly play the third phrase. Measures 9 and 10 are tricky because of the skip between G and E, the new note A, and also because rhythm is different.	To bring out beautiful shape of this piece, add *forte* dynamic to third phrase and *mezzo forte* to fourth phrase.

Supplementary Books:

Practice Games
Listen & Respond pgs. 16-17

Piano Technique
Mirage pgs. 19 & 22

Music Flash Cards – Set A
Pink #16, #17
Yellow #32

New Concepts: Dynamic shading	**Review:** 2nds, 3rds, 4ths
	Legato

Touch & Sound: ⟍ *Crescendo*

⟋ *Decrescendo*

Prepare	Practice	Perform
  While listening to *No One To Walk With*, student slides finger along slurs gently lifting wrist at end of each phrase. Ask student: "What is the mood of this piece?" "Can you tell a story from the picture?"	Student plays first two measures slowly with dynamic shading indicated while passing sound between hands.	Student plays piece in a slow, melancholy tempo, paying close attention to dynamics of each phrase. Small hands may use third finger on the last note marked *forte*.

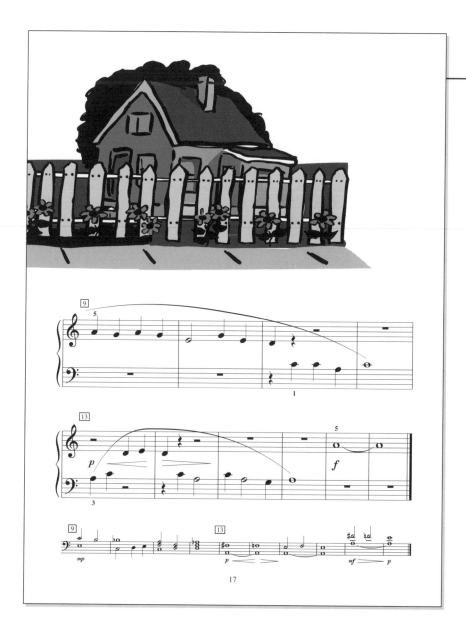

New Concepts:	None, review piece	Review:	*Legato*
			Parallel thumbs on C and D
Touch & Sound:	Rotating wrist to play melodic 2nds and 3rds		

Prepare	Practice	Perform
 While listening to *Painted Rocking Horse*, student: 1) claps and counts rhythm with a natural pulse on beats one and three. 2) student sings lyrics to first two measures on each line, and teacher answers by singing lyrics to last two measures of each line.	Student plays two-measure question phrase and teacher plays two-measure answer phrase. Switch parts.	With a pencil, student adds expression throughout piece (⟨ ⟩) and plays *Painted Rocking Horse* with *crescendos* and *decrescendos* indicated by student.

When the sky is cloud - y, you and I can play,

rock - ing through a gloom - y, rain - y day.

Supplementary Books:

Practice Games

Theory Workbook

Piano Technique

Notespeller

New Concepts:	None, review piece	Review:	Middle C position
			Staccato

Touch & Sound: *Staccato* between hands

Prepare	Practice	Perform
While listening to *Tick Tock The Jazz Clock*, student:	Student compares m. 7-8 with m. 15-16, then slowly plays each two-measure section.	Student plays *Tick Tock The Jazz Clock* in a lively tempo with strong pulse on first beat of each measure.
1) finger-taps lines one and three on the piano cabinet with full arm weight.		
2) plays lines one and three on keyboard with a clean *staccato* sound. Make sure student supports L.H. fourth finger with an arched hand position.		

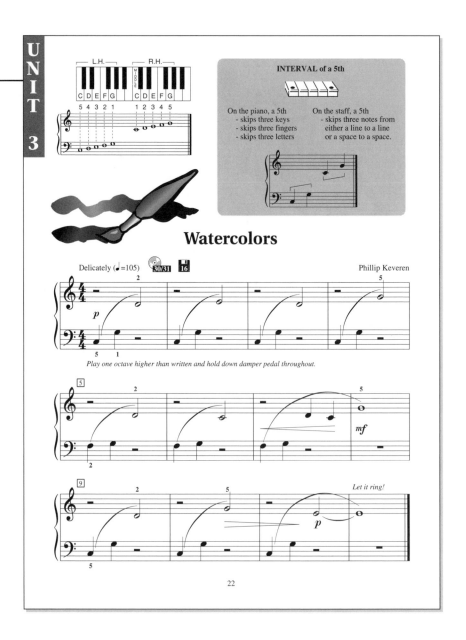

New Concepts:	Interval of a 5th	**Review:**	C position
			2nds, 3rds, 4ths
Touch & Sound:	Wrist motion: down, up, up		

Prepare	**Practice**	**Perform**
While listening to *Watercolors*, student places both hands in C position and repeats this wrist motion in dotted half-notes:	Add *crescendo* at the end of line two and *decrescendo* at the end of line three.	Student plays *Watercolors* one octave higher than written with damper pedal down throughout.

3/4 ♩. ↑ | ♩. ↑ :‖
          1 - 2 - 3   1 - 2 - 3

Ask student:
"How many 5ths are in this piece?"

"Does the R.H. play a 5th?"

To create a soft sound with good tone quality, student uses less arm weight, but full arm motion.

New Concepts:	Two-note slurs in R.H. with down-up motion	Review:	Two-note harmony between hands *D.C. al Fine*
Touch & Sound:	In m. 9-16, *legato* vs. *staccato* between hands		

Prepare	Practice	Perform
 While listening to *Circle Dance*, student: 1) places R.H. finger-tips on piano cabinet and repeats this wrist motion in quarter-notes:  2) finger-taps R.H. melody in lines one and two on piano cabinet using same *down-up-up* motion as above.	In the first two lines, student plays the first note of each measure hands together. Once this is mastered, student slowly plays music as written with a down/up motion on two-note slurs. In lines three and four, student plays with a soft, clean *staccato* touch in the L.H. Ask student to listen for crisp *staccato* on beats two and three of each measure.	Student plays *Circle Dance* with a smooth transition to main theme after *D.C. al Fine*.

Supplementary Books:

Practice Games
Listen & Respond pg. 26
Read & Discover pg. 27

Theory Workbook
Interval Bounce pg. 20

Music Flash Cards – Set A
Pink #18
Yellow #33

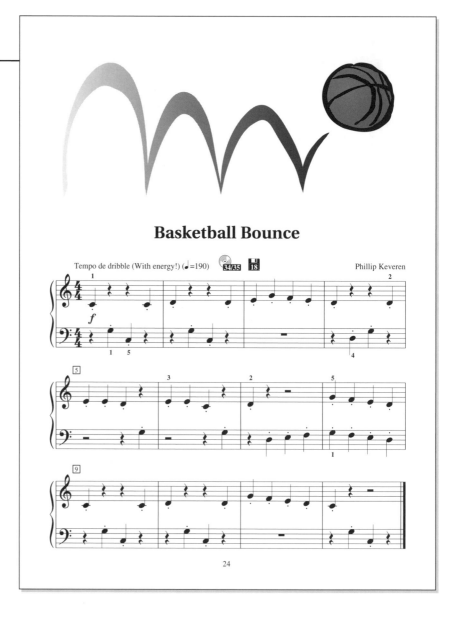

New Concepts:	None, review piece	Review:	Melodic intervals 2nd, 3rd, 4th, 5th
Touch & Sound:	*Staccato* between all intervals learned		

Prepare	**Practice**	**Perform**

While listening to *Basketball Bounce*, student taps R.H./L.H. rhythm on knees.
 	
Ask student:
"How many 5ths are in this piece?"
  – 4ths?
  – 3rds?
 	
"Where are the 4th and 5ths *between* the hands?"
	Student plays slow, detached *staccatos* with a strong pulse on the first beat of each measure.	Student plays *Basketball Bounce* using a bouncing wrist with full arm weight.

Supplementary Books:

Theory Workbook
It's A Tie! pg. 21

Piano Technique
Handbells pgs. 31-32

Notespeller
Back To The Scrambler pg. 18

New Concepts:	*8va - - ¬*		Review:	*Allegro* tempo marking
				Harmonic L.H. accompaniment
Touch & Sound:	*Legato*			$\frac{3}{4}$ time signature

Prepare	Practice	Perform
While listening to *Allegro*, student claps and counts rhythm of the melody. Ask student: "How long are the phrases in this piece?" "How many ties are in this piece?"	Student plays R.H. melody, placing a natural pulse on m. 1-3-5 and 7 to help shape the phrase. Student practices switching octaves in R.H. by bouncing 3rd finger back and forth from treble E to high E.	Student plays *Allegro* in a lively tempo, using less arm weight in the L.H. to balance the sound between melody and accompaniment.

New Concepts:	*Fortissimo* **ff**	**Review:**	
	8va - - -		*Legato* and *staccato*
Touch & Sound:	Playing with full arm weight		within one phrase

Prepare	**Practice**	**Perform**
  While listening to *Great News!*, student points and says note names. Ask student: "How many times do you see the pattern G G C C?" "How many times do you see the pattern G E G G?" (Be sure to check both clefs.)	Student slowly plays line four, making a smooth transition from melodic to harmonic intervals. Drop arm weight equally onto each key so all notes in harmonic intervals sound at exactly the same time.	Play *Great News!* with full arm weight and especially full arm motion on the *fortissimo* section. Students enjoy polytonal chord in measures 14 and 15.

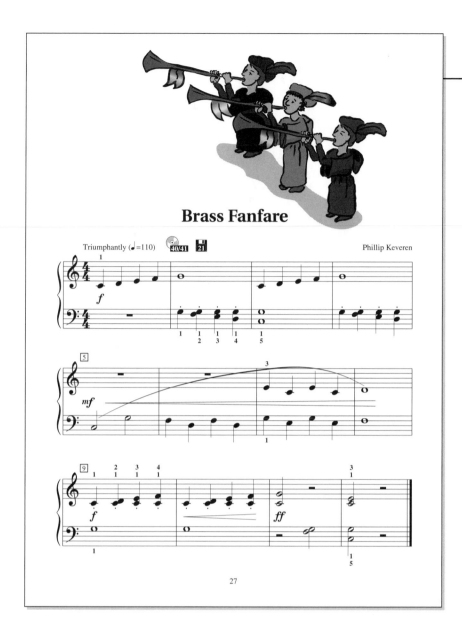

Supplementary Books:

Practice Games
  Listen & Respond pg. 29
  Imagine & Create pg. 29

Notespeller
  Brass Fanfare pg. 19

New Concepts:	None, review piece	Review:	*Crescendo* ▬▬▬
			Consecutive intervals
Touch & Sound:	*Staccato* on all harmonic		2nds, 3rds, 4ths, 5ths
	intervals learned		

Prepare	Practice	Perform
While listening to *Brass Fanfare*, student plays L.H. of line one and then R.H. of line two.	This piece features two distinct wrist motions.	Student plays *Brass Fanfare* with a dramatic *crescendo* starting at measure five to the end of the piece.
The student's wrist bounces lightly on each harmonic interval and fingers rebound naturally as they come to rest on the keys.	The *staccato* harmonic intervals in lines one and three are played with a down/up wrist motion.	
	The *legato* melodic intervals in line two are played with a side to side rocking motion as weight is transferred from finger to finger.	

Supplementary Books:

Theory Workbook
Sharps pg. 22

Piano Solos
Tribal Celebration pgs. 14-15

Music Flash Cards – Set A
Pink #20

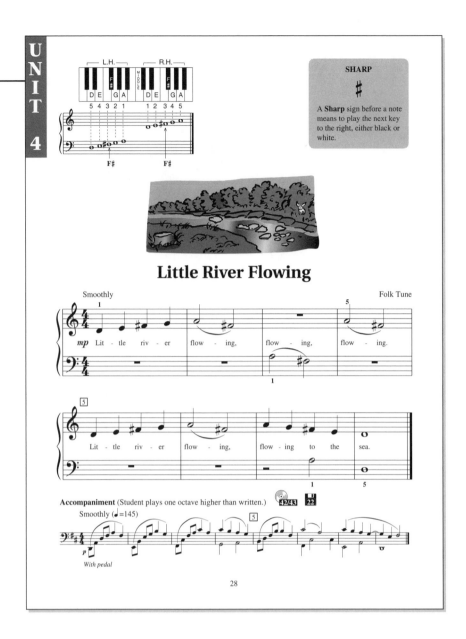

New Concepts:	D Major position	Review:	Two-note slurs
	New note, F♯		
Touch & Sound:	Wrist motion:		
	Down, up on two-note slurs		

Prepare	**Practice**	**Perform**
While listening to *Little River Flowing*, student sings lyrics with emphasis on FLOW-ing.	Slide student's hand position slightly toward piano fallboard so that the 3rd fingers rest naturally on the F♯ in each hand.	Student plays *Little River Flowing* with a clear down/up wrist motion on two-note slurs.

Quiet Thoughts

H. Berens
(1826 1880)
Op. 62
Adapted by Fred Kern

When a sharp appears before a note,
it remains sharp for one entire measure.

Accompaniment (Student plays one octave higher than written.)
Andante (♩=120)

29

New Concepts:	None, review piece	**Review:**	D Major position
			Sharp ♯
Touch & Sound:	In m. 7-8, parallel 6ths between hands		*Decrescendo*

Prepare	**Practice**	**Perform**
While listening to *Quiet Thoughts*, student claps and counts this rhythm pattern: 	Student slowly plays m. 7 and 8 carefully, studying direction of steps and skips. Student plays m. 1-2 and m. 3-4, noting the similar interval patterns. Student plays m. 5 and m. 6, noting the similar patterns.	When playing *Quiet Thoughts*, student adds a slight *crescendo* then *decrescendo* in m. 1-2 and then again in m. 3-4.

Supplementary Books:

Theory Workbook
Listening To Form –
Is It A Or B? pg. 23

Notespeller
The Star Quest Ride pgs. 20-21

Piano Solos
Take It Slow pgs. 18-19

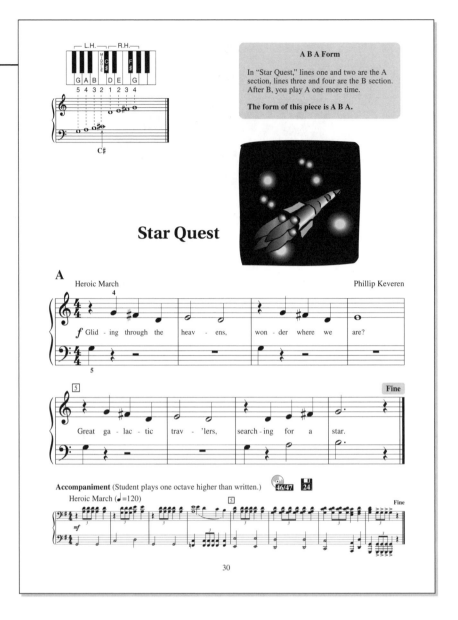

New Concepts:	A B A form	Review:	D.C. al Fine
	New note C♯		Crescendo
Touch & Sound:	Smoothly passing melody between the hands. Sudden dynamic change		

Prepare	Practice	Perform
While listening to *Star Quest*, student taps and counts rhythm. Ask student: "What other measures are exactly like the first?"	**A Section** Student reads and plays first two measures of lines one and two and teacher answers by playing last two measures of each line. Switch parts. **B Section** Student plays B section *legato* with less arm weight. Measure 12 is student's first experience with overlapping rhythm: R.H. whole-notes and L.H. half note.	Student plays *Star Quest* as written with *subito* dynamic change to *piano* in B section.

B

New Concepts:	New note, B♭		Review:	*mp*, *mf*, *f*
	Syncopated tied note			
Touch & Sound:	Harmony in 3rds between hands			

Prepare	Practice	Perform
While listening to *A Little Latin*, student claps and counts rhythm. This piece introduces syncopated rhythm with tied quarter notes into last measure.	Ask student: "How are measures 1 and 2 similar to measures 5 and 6?" "How are measures 5 and 6 similar to measures 7 and 8?" This piece becomes a quick study once student recognizes similar note patterns.	Student plays *A Little Latin* with terraced dynamics *mp* – *mf* – *f* from beginning to end.

Supplementary Books:

Practice Games
Listen & Respond pg. 34
Read & Discover pg. 34
Imagine & Create pg. 35

Music Flash Cards – Set A
Pink #22

New Concepts:	New note, E♭	**Review:**	Harmony in 3rds
	Accent >		
	Enharmonic notes D♯ and E♭		
Touch & Sound:	Melody overlaps L.H. harmony notes		

Prepare	Practice	Perform
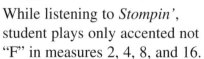 While listening to *Stompin'*, student plays only accented not "F" in measures 2, 4, 8, and 16. Student supports L.H. 5th finger with an arched hand when playing accents.	This is student's first experience with enharmonic notes E♭ and D♯. When playing D♯ to E, show student how to slide R.H. slightly toward piano fallboard so that 2nd finger falls naturally on the black key. Measures 9 and 11 feature overlapping rhythm with L.H. whole notes and R.H. half notes.	For fun, ask student to play entire piece and stomp foot on each accented note.

First Light

New Concepts:	*Ritard.*	**Review:**	*Decrescendo*

Touch & Sound: In m. 11 and 23, R.H. counter melody

Review: *Decrescendo*
3/4 time signature
Flat ♭

Prepare	Practice	Perform
 While listening to *First Light*, student claps this rhythm pattern:  Ask student: "How many phrases are in this piece?" "How long are the phrases in this piece?"	Student carefully studies the fingering and stepping motion in m. 2-3, and m. 5-6, then slowly plays these challenging measures until they are mastered.	Student plays *First Light*, adding *ritard.* in last measures of the piece.

35

New Concepts:	Natural ♮	**Review:**	*8va - - - ¬*
	R.H. crosses over L.H.		*mp* – *f*
Touch & Sound:	Alternating two-note slurs		Sharp ♯, Flat ♭
	between hands		

Prepare	Practice	Perform
  While listening to *Inspector Hound*, student finger-taps piece on piano cabinet. (Entire piece uses only fingers 2-3 in each hand.)	Student reads and plays *Inspector Hound*, moving R.H. up one octave at beginning of line two to prepare for *8va* in measure 7, and then moving R.H. down three octaves at beginning of line three to prepare for low "D" on last measure.	Dynamic changes from *mezzo piano* to *forte* help to make piece very sneaky sounding!

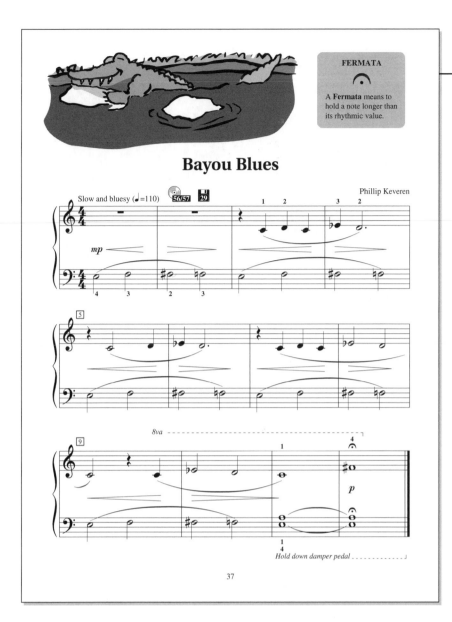

Bayou Blues

Phillip Keveren

Slow and bluesy (♩=110)

37

Supplementary Books:

Practice Games
  Listen & Respond pg. 37
  Read & Discover pg. 37

Theory Workbook
  Symbol Road pg. 28

Notespeller
  The Submarine Ride pg. 25

Piano Solos
  On Fourth Avenue pgs. 26-27

Music Flash Cards – Set A
  Pink #25
  Yellow #36

New Concepts:	Fermata ⌒	**Review:** <img crescendo/decrescendo>
		8va - - ¬
Touch & Sound:	L.H. *ostinato* with *legato* touch	Sharp ♯, Natural ♮

Prepare	Practice	Perform
While listening to *Bayou Blues*, student:	Ask student to write in the beats for each R.H. phrase, then play R.H. only while counting aloud.	Student slowly plays hands together, lining up tricky rhythm between the hands.
1) plays L.H. *ostinato* as written with *crescendo* and *decrescendo* expression.	The R.H. always plays C D E♭, but never in the same order or in the same rhythm. Practice m. 2, m. 4, m. 6, m. 8 and m. 10 hands together.	*Hint:* The F♯ in L.H. and E♭ in R.H. always play together.

2) counts and claps R.H. melody line.	Ask the student:
	  – Which measures are the same?
	  – Which measures are different?	

FERMATA ⌒
A **Fermata** means to hold a note longer than its rhythmic value.

Music Flash Cards – Set A
Yellow #37, #38

New Concepts: In m. 9-12, two-note slurs with an upbeat

Touch & Sound: 4-measure phrases with rise and fall in each slur

Review: Upbeat
Andante
Rit.

Prepare	Practice	Perform
While listening to *Serenade*, student claps and counts rhythm. Ask student: "How many phrases are in this piece?" "How many phrases have upbeats (pick-up notes)?"	This piece is an excellent study in shaping phrases. Student gives a natural pulse to odd numbered measures (1-3-5-7, etc.).	Student plays *Serenade* with dynamic shading indicated on second page. Playing upbeats with a lilt will keep melody moving forward.

A sharp before a note
lasts for only one measure.

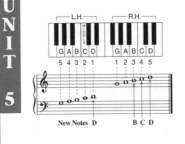

Summer Evenings

New Concepts:	G Major position	**Review:**	*mf – mp*
	New treble notes B C D		*Rit.*
	Ledger line D		*Legato*
Touch & Sound:	Parallel 6ths between hands		
	4-measure phrases		

Prepare	**Practice**	**Perform**
  While listening to *Summer Evenings*, student: 1) claps and counts rhythm. 2) points and says R.H. note names. This is student's first experience in G position. Ask student: "How many ledger-line Ds are in this piece?"	In m. 13-16, add interest to repeated notes by placing emphasis on the downbeat of each measure. Student plays m. 15-16 as an echo of m. 13-14.	Student plays *Summer Evenings* with delicate *ritard.* in last two measures of piece.

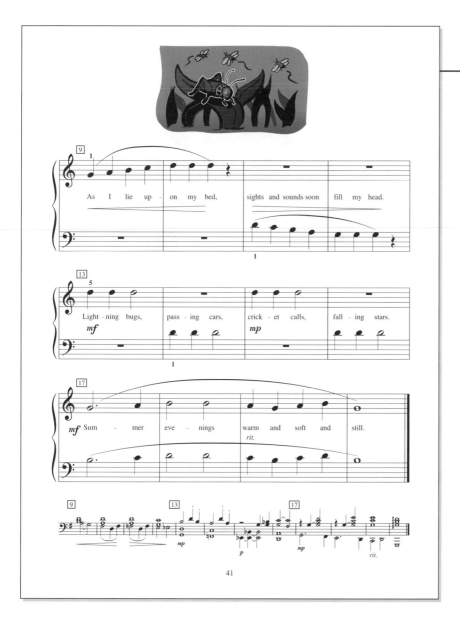

As I lie up - on my bed, sights and sounds soon fill my head.

Light - ning bugs, pass - ing cars, crick - et calls, fall - ing stars.

mf

mp

Sum - mer eve - nings warm and soft and still.

mf

rit.

mp

p

mp

rit.

41

Theory Workbook
  Spike Is Puzzled! pg. 31

**My Own Song
On G A B C D**

Place both hands on G A B C D. Listen and feel the pulse as your teacher plays the accompaniment below.

With your right hand, play G A B C D. Experiment by playing D C B A G. Mix the letters any way you want and make up your own song!

With your left hand, play G A B C D. Experiment by playing D C B A G. Again, mix the letters any way you want and make up another song!

Have fun!

Accompaniment 62 32
Jazz Waltz (♩=170)

Repeat as necessary | *Last time*

42

New Concepts:	Improvising in G Major position	**Review:**	Treble clef notes B C D

Prepare	**Practice**	**Perform**
62 32 While listening to *My Own Song On G A B C D*, student taps quarter notes, then dotted half-notes.	Student improvises in G Major five-finger pattern in one or more octaves up and down keyboard.	Encourage student to improvise freely, using one or both hands and with one or more note values.

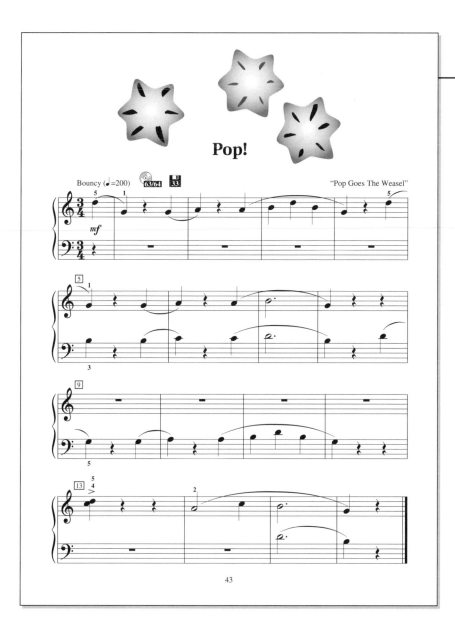

New Concepts:	None, review piece	**Review:**	Accent >
			Upbeat
Touch & Sound:	Two-note slurs starting on		G Major position
	an up-beat (weak beat)		Treble notes B C D

Prepare	Practice	Perform
While listening to *Pop!*, student points and says notes.	Student plays slurred phrases with a down-up wrist motion. Line two is familiar to student since it is the same pattern of parallel 6ths between the hands introduced in *Summer Evenings*.	<u>Extra for Experts</u> Student plays *Pop!* with the Instrumental Accompaniment for *My Own Song On G A B C D*.

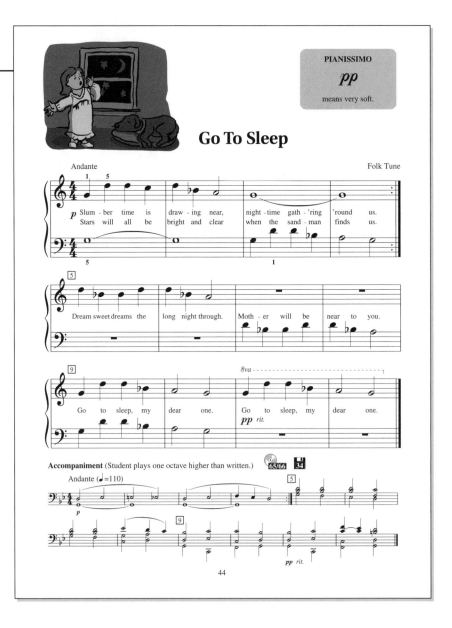

New Concepts:	*Pianissimo* **pp**	Review:	Flat ♭
	G minor position		*Ritard.*
Touch & Sound:	Playing 3rd fingers on B♭		*8va - - ¬*
			Repeat sign :‖

Prepare	Practice	Perform
While listening to *Go To Sleep*, student claps rhythm of melody.	Teacher plays the first two measures of each line while student answers by playing the last two measures of each line. Switch parts.	Student plays *Go To Sleep* with very little arm weight, using full arm motion on each note to produce a good tone quality.

Jig

Supplementary Books:

Practice Games
Listen & Respond pg. 39

Theory Workbook
Upbeat pg. 35
Rhythm Detective pg. 36

Notespeller
The Roller Coaster pgs. 30-31

Piano Solos
School Is Out! pgs. 30-31

Music Flash Cards – Set B
Pink #78

New Concepts:	Two-note upbeat	**Review:**	Harmonic 4ths and 5ths
	1st and 2nd endings		in G Major position
Touch & Sound:	L.H. harmonic intervals		$\boldsymbol{f}$
	played with a loose wrist		Ledger note D

Prepare	**Practice**	**Perform**
While listening to *Jig*, student plays ledger-line D with L.H. thumb in this rhythm:	Student plays melody line only by first omitting all L.H. harmonic intervals.	Student plays *Jig* in a light, brisk tempo, with a light *staccato* touch on harmonic intervals.
	Once melody is mastered, add harmonic intervals in L.H. and play piece as written.	

New Concepts:	New bass note A♭	Review:	A B A form
			$f - mf - f$
Touch & Sound:	L.H. position change in m. 9-12		

Prepare	Practice	Perform
While listening to *Go For The Gold*, student counts and taps L.H./R.H. rhythm on knees.	Student plays first two measures of each line and teacher answers with the last two measures of each line. Student slowly plays m. 3 and 4 hands together, carefully reading skips and steps. *Hint:* Note the R.H./L.H. matching intervals in m. 3: skip up, step down on beats 3 and 4. Then, on the downbeat of m. 4, both hands play finger #2.	Student plays *Go For The Gold* in a stately tempo, using full arm weight in the *forte* section. Ask student to name the mood, or emotion, of this piece.

47

AWARD
CERTIFICATE

HAS SUCCESSFULLY COMPLETED
HAL LEONARD PIANO LESSONS,
BOOK TWO
AND
IS HEREBY PROMOTED TO
BOOK THREE.

TEACHER   DATE

HAL•LEONARD®

The Hal Leonard Student Piano Library

Lesson Planning Charts   pgs. 50-65

This Lesson Planning Chart divides Book 2 of the
Hal Leonard Student Piano Library into 32 *Learning Modules*.
Lesson Planning Charts dividing Books 3, 4, and 5 into 32 *Learning Modules*
each, are also included.

- Younger students may average one module per week.
- Older students may average two modules per week.

Imagine & Create Activities   pgs. 66-72

As featured in *Piano Practice Games Book 2*.

BOOK TWO	UNIT 1 Module 1	Module 2	Module 3	Module 4	Module 5	UNIT 2 Module 6	Module 7	Module 8
PIANO LESSONS & GAMES	Reflection pg. 4 My Own Song On C D E F G pg. 5 Ode To Joy pg. 6	Carmen's Tune pg. 7 *Piano Games pg. 3*	Andantino pg. 8 *Piano Games pgs. 4-5*	Big Ben pg. 9 Please, No Bees! pg. 10 *Piano Games pg. 6*	Clapping Song pg. 11	Hoedown pg. 12 *Piano Games pg. 8*	*Piano Games pg. 7* Sunlight Through The Trees pg. 13	*Piano Games pg. 9* Bingo pg. 14 *Piano Games pg. 13*
THEORY	The Grand Staff – A Musical Map pg. 2 Drawing Notes And Stems pg. 3	Drawing Notes On The Staff pg. 4 Playing On C D E F G pg. 5	Rhythm Detective pg. 6	Note Name Review pg. 7 Harmonic Or Melodic? pg. 8 Harmonic 2nds And 3rds pg. 9	Legato Or Staccato? pg. 10 Drawing Legato And Staccato Marks pg. 11	4ths pg. 12	Intervalasaurus pg. 13	Upbeat Melodies pg. 14
TECHNIQUE	Take Another Look pg. 5 Rope Bridge pgs. 6, 7 & 8	See-Saw pgs. 6, 7 & 9	Red Light, Green Light pgs. 10, 11 & 12	Bee Cha-Cha pgs. 10, 11 & 13		Tiptoe pgs. 14, 15 & 16	Windchimes pgs. 14, 15 & 17	Out To Sea pgs. 18-21
NOTESPELLER	At The Ticket Booth pg. 2 *Piano Park* Tokens pg. 3 The Half-Note Express pg. 4	The Train Ride pg. 5	The Canoe Ride pgs. 6-7	Name The Canoes! pg. 8 The Ferris Wheel pg. 9		Snow Cones pg. 10	A Treasure Hunt pg. 11	
SOLOS		Magnet March pg. 3	Song Of The Orca pgs. 4-5		The Macaroni Cha-Cha pgs. 6-7		The Stream pgs. 8-9	
FLASH CARDS	Set A – White #8, bass "C" #9, bass "D" #10, bass "E" Set A – Yellow #5, whole rest	Set A – Yellow #28, rhythm	Set A – Pink #14, slur (*legato*)	Set A – Pink #27, 2nds #28, 2nds #29, 3rds #30, 3rds Set A – Yellow #29, rhythm	Set A – Pink #15, *staccato*	Set A – Pink #31, 4ths #32, 4ths	Set A – Yellow #30, rhythm	

BOOK TWO

UNIT 3 spans Module 13.

Section	Module 9	Module 10	Module 11	Module 12	Module 13	Module 14	Module 15	Module 16
PIANO LESSONS & GAMES	*Piano Games* pgs. 10-11; **Travelling Along The Prairie** pg. 15, *Piano Games* pg. 14	**No One To Walk With** pgs. 16-17, *Piano Games* pgs. 16-17	**Painted Rocking Horse** pgs. 18-19, *Piano Games* pg. 18; *Piano Games* pg. 15	**Tick Tock The Jazz Clock** pgs. 20-21, *Piano Games* pgs. 19-20	**Watercolors** pg. 22, *Piano Games* pg. 22	*Piano Games* pg. 21; **Circle Dance** pg. 23, *Piano Games* pgs. 24-25; **Basketball Bounce** pg. 24, *Piano Games* pgs. 26-27	**Allegro** pg. 25	**Great News!** pg. 26, *Piano Games* pg. 28
THEORY	**Measuring Upbeats** pg. 15		**Dynamic Detective** pg. 16	**"W"Rong Rhythms** pg. 17	**Beeline To The Intervals** pg. 18	**Ties Or Slurs?** pg. 19	**Interval Bounce** pg. 20; **It's A Tie!** pg. 21	
TECHNIQUE		**Mirage** pgs. 18, 19 & 22		**Prancing** pgs. 18,19 & 23		**Can You...?** pgs. 24, 25 & 26; **You Can!** pgs. 24, 25 & 27	**Outside-In** pgs. 24, 25 & 28; **Inside-Out** pgs. 24, 25 & 29	
NOTESPELLER	**The Airplane Ride** pgs. 12-13		**The Magic Show** pg. 14	**Go Carts** pg. 15	**The Scrambler** pg. 16	**The Queen's Castle** pg. 17	**Back To The Scrambler** pg. 18	
SOLOS	**Leaps And Bounds** pg. 10	**Tender Dialogue** pg. 11				**Dance Of The Court Jester** pgs. 12-13		
FLASH CARDS	Set A – White #20, treble "A"; Set A – Yellow #31, rhythm	Set A – Pink #16, *crescendo* #17, *decrescendo*; Set A – Yellow #32, rhythm			Set A – Pink #33, 5ths #34, 5ths		Set A – Pink #18, *8va*; Set A – Yellow #33, rhythm	Set A – Pink #19, *fortissimo*; Set A – Yellow #34, rhythm

BOOK TWO

BOOK TWO	Module 17	UNIT 4 Module 18	Module 19	Module 20	Module 21	Module 22	Module 23	Module 24
PIANO LESSONS & GAMES	Brass Fanfare pg. 27 *Piano Games* *pg. 29*	Little River Flowing pg. 28 Quiet Thoughts pg. 29 *Piano Games* *pgs. 30-31*	Star Quest pgs. 30-31	A Little Latin pg. 32 *Piano Games* *pg. 32*	Stompin' pg. 33 *Piano Games* *pg. 34*	First Light pgs. 34-35 *Piano Games* *pg. 33*	*Piano Games* *pg. 35* Inspector Hound pg. 36 *Piano Games* *pg. 36*	Bayou Blues pg. 37 *Piano Games* *pg. 37*
THEORY		Sharps pg. 22	Listening To Form – Is It A Or B? pg. 23	Flats pg. 24	Ritard (*rit.*) pg. 25	Naturals pg. 26 Sign Quest pg. 27	Symbol Road pg. 28	
TECHNIQUE	Handbells pgs. 30, 31 & 32	A-Rest pgs. 30, 31 & 33	Meditation pgs. 34, 35 & 36	Too Cool! pgs. 34, 35 & 37				
NOTESPELLER	Brass Fanfare pg. 19		The Star Quest Ride pgs. 20-21	Star Quest Spaceships pg. 22		Haunted House pg. 23	The Sky Ride pg. 24	The Submarine Ride pg. 25
SOLOS		Tribal Celebration pgs. 14-15	The Accompaniment pgs. 16-17	Take It Slow pgs. 18-19	Viva La Rhumba! pgs. 20-21	Grandmother's Lace pgs. 22-23	Those Creepy Crawly Things... pgs. 24-25	On Fourth Avenue pgs. 26-27
FLASH CARDS		Set A – Pink #20, sharp		Set A – Pink #21, flat Set A – Yellow #35, rhythm	Set A – Pink #22, accent	Set A – Pink #23, *ritard.*	Set A – Pink #25, natural	Set A – Pink #25, fermata Set A – Yellow #36, rhythm

Module 25	UNIT 5 Module 26	Module 27	Module 28	Module 29	Module 30	Module 31	Module 32	BOOK TWO
Serenade pgs. 38-39	My Own Song On G A B C D pg. 42 Summer Evenings pgs. 40-41	Pop! pgs. 43	Go To Sleep pg. 44	Piano Games pg. 38 Jig pg. 45 Piano Games pg. 39	Go For The Gold pgs. 46-47		Piano Games pg. 40	PIANO LESSONS & GAMES
	The Grand Staff – Playing On B C D pg. 29 Ledger Lines pg. 30 Spike Is Puzzled! pg. 31	Octave Sign pg. 32 G A B C D Mysteries pg. 33	Dynamic Play pg. 34	Upbeat pg. 35 Rhythm Detective pg. 36	Interval Food pg. 37	Interval Roundup pg. 38	Relay Review pg. 39	THEORY
	Meet In The Middle pgs. 38-39			Scattered Showers pgs. 38 & 40				TECHNIQUE
	The Water Slide pgs. 26-27	Bumper Cars pg. 28	The Merry- Go-Round pg. 29	The Roller Coaster pgs. 30-31	Celebration pg. 32			NOTESPELLER
		Goofy Gadget pgs. 28-29		School Is Out! pgs. 30-31				SOLOS
Set A – Yellow #37, rhythm #38, rhythm	Set A – White #21, treble "B" #22, treble "C" #23, high "D" #33, middle ledger "D"	Set A – Yellow #39, rhythm	Set A – Pink #26, pianissimo Set B – Pink #53, dynamics	Set B – Pink #78, upbeat	Set A – Yellow #40, rhythm			FLASH CARDS

BOOK THREE

BOOK THREE	UNIT 1 Module 1	Module 2	Module 3	Module 4	UNIT 2 Module 5	Module 6	Module 7	Module 8
PIANO LESSONS & GAMES	Little River Flowing pg. 4 / Dakota Melody pg. 5 / *Piano Games pg. 3*	Hiccups In School pg. 6 / *Piano Games pg. 4*	Little Bird pg. 7 / *Piano Games pg. 6*	*Piano Games pg. 5* / Lullaby pg. 8	Lavender Mood pgs. 10-11 / *Piano Games pg. 10* / Shortbread Boogie pg. 9	Casey Jones pgs. 12-13 / *Piano Games pgs. 7-9*	*Piano Games pg. 11* / Take Me Out To The Ball Game pgs. 14-15 / *Piano Games pgs. 12-13*	Harvest Song pg. 16
THEORY	Eighth Notes pg. 2 / More Stems And Beams pg. 3 / Dakota Drummer pg. 4	Hiccups! pg. 5 / The Grand Staff – Playing On G A B C D pg. 6	Bird Notes pg. 7		6ths pg. 8 / Musical Blossoms pg. 9 / Pop Quiz! pg. 10	All Aboard pg. 11	Which Clef? pg. 12	
TECHNIQUE	Procession pg. 5	Rebound pgs. 6, 7 & 8		Horn Choir pgs. 6, 7 & 9		E-I-E-I-O pgs. 10, 11 & 12		Rubber Band pgs. 10, 11 & 13
NOTESPELLER	Rhythm Train Terminal pgs. 2-3	Half-Note Hotel pg. 4	A Cab Ride To The Music City Zoo pg. 5		Dinner At Six pg. 6	Who Wants To Be A Musician? pg. 7		
SOLOS			Racing Toward Home pg. 3			Blues Prelude pgs. 4-5	Fiesta March pgs. 6-7	Tap Dance pgs. 8-9
FLASH CARDS	Set B – Yellow #42, eighth notes #47, 2/4 time #52, rhythm #53, rhythm	Set A – White #5, low "G" #6, low "A" #7, low "B" / Set B – Pink #73, *sempre*	Set B – Yellow #54, rhythm	Set B – Yellow #55, rhythm	Set A – Pink #35, 6ths #36, 6ths / Set B – Pink #58, interval #57, harmonic interval #63, melodic interval	Set A – White #24, high "E" / Set B – Yellow #56, rhythm		

BOOK THREE

	Module 9	Module 10	UNIT 3 Module 11	Module 12	Module 13	Module 14	UNIT 4 Module 15	Module 16	BOOK THREE
PIANO LESSONS & GAMES	Spring pg. 17 / *Piano Games* pgs. 14-15	Bounces pg. 18 / *Piano Games* pg. 16	All Through The Night pg. 19 / *Piano Games* pg. 17 / The Last Word pg. 20	Monkey Business pg. 21 / Dixieland Jam pg. 22 / *Piano Games* pg. 18	Inchworm Waltz pg. 23	Setting Sun pgs. 24-25 / *Piano Games* pgs. 20-21 / *Piano Games* pg. 19	My Own Song In C Major pg. 27 / Barefoot On A Hot Sidewalk pg. 27	Quadrille pg. 28 / *Piano Games* pg. 22	
THEORY	Note These Flower Boxes pg. 13		Rhythm Wheel pg. 14 / The Last Word! pg. 15 / Flags, Dots, And Beams pg. 16	Two Names – Same Key! pg. 17 / Half Steps pg. 18		Whole Steps pg. 19 / Half Or Whole? pg. 20	Stepping Out pg. 21 / C Major Five-Finger Patterns pg. 22	Switching Gears pg. 23	
TECHNIQUE		Shifting Gears pgs. 14, 15 & 16	Habañera pgs. 14, 15 & 17		Formal Gardens pgs. 18, 19 & 20	The Aquarium pgs. 18, 19 & 21		Over And Over pgs. 22, 23 & 24	
NOTESPELLER	The J.S. Bach Building pgs. 8-9	Treble-Clef Café pg. 10		Grand Staff Stadium pg. 11		Steppin' Out In Harmony Village pgs. 12-13	The Beethoven Bridge pg. 14		
SOLOS		Lullaby Angel pgs. 10-11				Leap Frog pgs. 12-13			
FLASH CARDS	Set A – White #25, high "F" / #25, high "G" / Set B – Yellow #57, rhythm		Set A – White #30, middle ledger "B" / Set B – Yellow #44, dotted quarter note / #43, eighth note / #58, rhythm	Set A – White #32, middle ledger "E"	Set B – White #59, rhythm	Set B – Pink #61, *loco* / #45, *a tempo* / #76, *tempo* / Set B – Yellow #60, rhythm	Set B – White #43, C major pattern / #46, C major triad		

BOOK THREE	Module 17	Module 18	Module 19	Module 20	Module 21	UNIT 5 Module 22	Module 23	Module 24
PIANO LESSONS & GAMES	My Own Song In G Major pg. 29 Gravitational Pull pg. 29	Scherzo pgs. 30-31 *Piano Games* *pg. 23*	My Own Song In F Major pg. 32 Fall In Line pg. 32	The Fife 'n' Horn pg. 33 *Piano Games* *pg. 24*	Chorale pg. 34 *Piano Games* *pgs. 26-27*	My Own Song In A Minor pg. 37 Minor Dance pg. 37 *Piano Games* *pgs. 25* Walk Around The Block pg. 35 *Piano Games* *pg. 28*	Romance pgs. 38-39 *Piano Games* *pgs. 29-30*	My Own Song In E Minor pg. 40 Sad Melody pg. 40
THEORY			More Major Five-Finger Patterns pg. 24	Every Triad Has A Root! pg. 25	Adding The Damper Pedal pg. 26 Triad Checkerboard pg. 27	A-maze-ing Rhythms pg. 28 Walk Around The Patterns pg. 29	Minor Five-Finger Patterns pg. 30 Minor Triads pg. 31	
TECHNIQUE					Quiet Moments pgs. 22, 23 & 25		Peanut Butter pgs. 26, 27 & 28	
NOTESPELLER	Music City Ferry-Boat Tour pg. 15				The Haydn Planetarium pg. 16			Staccato Island Freeway pg. 17
SOLOS	Awesome Adventure pgs. 14-15					The Banjo Picker pgs. 16-17		
FLASH CARDS	Set B – White #56, G major pattern #56, G major triad	Set B – Pink #50, *D.S. al Fine* Set B – Yellow #61, rhythm #62, rhythm	Set B – White #69, F major pattern #72, F major triad	Set B – Yellow #63, rhythm		Set B – White #49, A minor pattern #52, A minor triad		Set B – White #62, E minor pattern #65, E minor triad

BOOK THREE

	Module 25	Module 26	Module 27	Module 28	Module 29	Module 30	Module 31	Module 32	BOOK THREE
PIANO LESSONS & GAMES	Fierce Heart pg. 41 / *Piano Games* pgs. 31-32	My Own Song In D Minor pg. 42 / Street Fair pg. 42	Medieval Muse pg. 43	Floating pg. 44 / *Piano Games* pg. 34	Joy pg. 45 / *Piano Games* pg. 37 / *Piano Games* pgs. 35-36	Fresh Start pgs. 46-47 / *Piano Games* pgs. 38-39	*Piano Games* pg. 40		
THEORY		Name The Five-Finger Pattern pg. 32	Major And Minor Leagues pg. 33 / Musical Flight Patterns pg. 34	Rainbow Of Patterns pg. 35	Triad Jumble pg. 36 / Bear's Favorite Chord Song pg. 37	Spike Is Puzzled! pg. 38		Musical Riddles pg. 39	
TECHNIQUE	Jam pgs. 26, 27 & 29			Cut And Paste pgs. 30, 31 & 32	Joshua's Dance pgs. 30, 31 & 33 / Sleep-Over pgs. 34, 35 & 36	Skipping Stones pgs. 34, 35 & 37			
NOTESPELLER	The Wonder Wheel pg. 18		Tune -Time Trolley pg. 19		Flags Along Sonatina Street pg. 20		Symphony Park pg. 21		
SOLOS	I Remember... pgs. 20-21		The Clockwork Ballerina pgs. 22-23		To The Magic Forest pgs. 24-25	The Winter Wind pgs. 26-27	Porcupine Pizzicato pgs. 28-29	Gestures pgs. 30-31	
FLASH CARDS		Set B – White #75, D minor pattern #78, D minor triad	Set B – Pink #49, *D.C. al Coda*		Set A – White #27, high ledger "A" #28, high ledger "B" #29, high ledger "C"	Set A – White #31, middle ledger "A" / Set B – Yellow #64, rhythm			

57

BOOK FOUR	UNIT 1 Module 1	Module 2	Module 3	Module 4	Module 5	UNIT 2 Module 6	Module 7	Module 8
PIANO LESSONS & GAMES	My Own Song In C Major And E Minor pg. 4 — Rustic Dance pg. 5 — *Piano Games* pg. 3	Carpet Ride pg. 6 — *Piano Games* pg. 4	My Own Song In G Major And E Minor pg. 7 — Mr. Banjo pg. 8 — *Piano Games* pg. 6	*Piano Games* pg. 5 — Morning Bells pg. 9 — *Piano Games* pg. 8	*Piano Games* pg. 7 — *Piano Games* pg. 9 — Ribbons pg. 10 — *Piano Games* pg. 10	Scale Preparation pg. 11 — Moving On Up – C Major Scale Pattern pg. 12 —	Calypso Cat pg. 13 — *Piano Games* pg. 11	Jig pg. 14 — *Piano Games* pg. 12
THEORY	The Reflecting Pool pg. 2 What Do You See (C)? pg. 3	Magic Major And Minor Carpets pg. 4 Be A Genie-us pg. 5	Pickin' Rests pg. 6		Hopscotch 7ths pg. 7 Ribbon Wrap-Up pg. 8		The Major Scale pg. 9 Flags, Dots and Beams pg. 10	3/8 and 6/8 Time pg. 11
TECHNIQUE	Major Minor pg. 5 Red Rover pgs. 6, 7 & 8	Get It Together pgs. 6, 7 & 9	Take It Away pgs. 10, 11 & 12	Bell Choir pgs. 10, 11 & 13	Silk And Satin pgs. 14, 15 & 16		Zip It! pgs. 14, 15 & 17	Bungee Cord pgs. 18, 19 & 20
NOTESPELLER						*Orchestra Hall pgs. 22-23 *These pages are found in *Notespeller for Piano Book 3*.		
SOLOS		El Torrito pg. 3		Porch Swing pg. 4	Stubborn Little Donkey pg. 5	Latin Logic pgs. 6-7	Spinning Daydreams pgs. 8-9	
FLASH CARDS		Set B – Yellow #65, rhythm	Set B – Yellow #45, eighth rest #66, rhythm			Set B – Pink #65, *moderato* Set B – White #44, C Major scale	Set B – Yellow #67, rhythm Set B – White #42, C Major, A minor	Set B – Yellow #48, 3/8 time #49, 6/8 time #68, rhythm #69, rhythm

	Module 9	Module 10	Module 11	UNIT 3 Module 12	Module 13	Module 14	Module 15	Module 16	BOOK FOUR
PIANO LESSONS & GAMES	Two-Four-Six-Eight pg. 16	*Piano Games* pg. 13 / Moving On Up – A Minor Scale pg. 19 / Allegro pg. 20 / *Piano Games* pg. 15	*Piano Games* pg. 14 / Etude pg. 21 / *Piano Games* pg. 16	Take It Easy pg. 22 / *Piano Games* pg. 18 / Close By pg. 23 / *Piano Games* pg. 19	Jumping Beans pg. 24 / *Piano Games* pg. 20 / *Piano Games* pg. 17	Relay Race pg. 25 / *Piano Games* pg. 21	A Minor Tango pg. 26 / *Piano Games* pg. 22	All The Pretty Little Horses pg. 27	
THEORY	Tied and Untied pg. 12 / Field Goal! pg. 13	The Minor Scale pg. 14	Ledger Line Notes Above The Bass Staff pg. 15	Primary Triads In C Major pg. 16 / Tie-ing It All Together pg. 17	A-maze-ing Octaves pg. 18 / Name This Tune pg. 19	Pop Quiz! pg. 20	Primary Triads In A Minor pg. 21 / Ledger Line Notes Below The Treble Staff pg. 22	Play Pool! pg. 23 / Sound Check pg. 27	
TECHNIQUE		Beethoven's Fifth – Not! pgs. 18, 19 & 21	Reaching pgs. 22, 23 & 24			Smooth Hand -Off pgs. 22, 23 & 25			
NOTESPELLER	*The World Art Museum pg. 24 / *These pages are found in *Notespeller for Piano Book 3*.				*Legato Lake Festival pg. 25	*Festival Games pg. 26	*Time To Eat! pg. 27		
SOLOS	Six Ate Beets pgs. 10-11	Scavenger Hunt pgs. 12-13	Northern Ode pgs. 14-15	Venetian Boat Song pgs. 16-17		The Dreamcatcher pgs. 18-19			
FLASH CARDS	Set B – Yellow #70, rhythm	Set B – White #50, A minor scale		Set B – Yellow #71, rhythm #72, rhythm / Set B – White #45, C Major cadence	Set B – Pink #56, *giocoso* #72, rhythm / Set B – Yellow #73, rhythm / Set B – White #46, #47, #48		Set B – Pink #46, *allegretto* / Set B – Yellow #50, Common Time	Set B – White #51, A minor cadence #52, #53, #54	

BOOK FOUR		UNIT 4					UNIT 5	
	Module 17	Module 18	Module 19	Module 20	Module 21	Module 22	Module 23	Module 24
PIANO LESSONS & GAMES	Joshua Fit The Battle Of Jericho pg. 28	**Moving On Up – G Major Scale** pg. 30 **Spanish Dance** pg. 31 *Piano Games pg. 23*	**True Blues** pg. 32 *Piano Games pg. 25*	*Piano Games pg. 24* **Blues For A Count** pg. 34 *Piano Games pg. 26*	**Doo Wop Ditty** pg. 35 *Piano Games pg. 28*	*Piano Games pg. 27* **Moving On Up – E Minor Scale** pg. 36 **Wandering** pg. 37 *Piano Games pg. 30*	**Ready To Rock!** pg. 38 *Piano Games pg. 31*	**The Bass Singer** pg. 39 *Piano Games pg. 30*
THEORY	**Mixing Meters** pg. 25 **Ledger Line Notes Below The Bass Staff** pg. 26	**The G Major Scale** pg. 27	**Common Time And Cut Time** pg. 28 **Rhythm Detective** pg. 29	**Triplet Magic Hat** pg. 30		**The E Minor Scale** pg. 31 **Scale Relay** pg. 32		
TECHNIQUE	**Hurry Up And Wait** pgs. 26, 27 & 28	**Tidal Lullaby** pgs. 26, 27 & 29	**Talkin' To My Left Hand** pgs. 30, 31 & 32	**Heading For Home** pgs. 30, 31 & 33		**Fitting In** pgs. 34, 35 & 36	**Low-Down** pgs. 34, 35 & 37	
NOTESPELLER		*4/4 Time Square pgs. 28-29 *These pages are found in *Notespeller for Piano Book 3*.			*Mozart Center For The Performing Arts pg. 30		*Melody Mall pg. 31	*Farewell pg. 32
SOLOS		**Easy Does It** pg. 20	**Bear Tracks** pg. 21		**Lyrical Prelude** pgs. 22-23	**Folk Dance** pgs. 24-25		**Boogie Blues** pgs. 26-27
FLASH CARDS	Set B – Yellow #72, rhythm	Set B – Pink #79, *vivace* Set B – White #55, G Major, E minor #57, G Major scale	Set B – Yellow #51, Cut Time #75, rhythm #76, rhythm	Set B – Yellow #46, triplet	Set B – Yellow #77, rhythm	Set B – Yellow #78, rhythm Set B – White #63, E minor scale	Set B – White #58, G Major cadence #57, #60, #61	

Module 25	Module 26	Module 27	Module 28	Module 29	Module 30	Module 31	Module 32	BOOK FOUR
On The Prowl pg. 40 *Piano Games* pg. 33	**Starry Night** pg. 41 *Piano Games* pg. 34	**Rhapsody** pgs. 42-43	**Longing** pg. 44 *Piano Games* pg. 36	*Piano Games* pg. 35 **Presto** pg. 45 *Piano Games* pg. 38	*Piano Games* pg. 37 **Allegro** pgs. 46-47 *Piano Games* pg. 39	*Piano Games* pg. 40		PIANO LESSONS & GAMES
Primary Triads In G Major And E Minor pg. 33	**Ledger Line Notes Above The Treble Staff** pg. 34 **Spike's Special Spelling Test** pg. 35	**Tie-ing It All Together** pg. 36	**Name The Triad** pg. 37	**Spike Is Puzzled!** pg. 38	**Musical Riddles** pg. 39			THEORY
	In A Swing pgs. 38, 39 & 40	**Beach Ball** pgs. 38, 39 & 41	**Kaleidoscope** pgs. 42, 43 & 44	**Rolling Down The Hill** pgs. 42, 43 & 45	**Horn Call** pgs. 46-47	**Scales** pg. 48		TECHNIQUE
								NOTESPELLER
	Secret Agent pgs. 28-29		**Capriccio** pgs. 30-31					SOLOS
Set B – Yellow #74, rhythm **Set B – White** #64, E minor cadence #64, #66, #67	**Set B – Pink** #51, *diminuendo* #68, *poco*		**Set B –Pink** #48, *con motto* **Set B – Yellow** #79, rhythm	**Set B – Pink** #70, *presto* **Set B – Yellow** #80, rhythm				FLASH CARDS

61

BOOK FIVE	UNIT 1 Module 1	Module 2	Module 3	Module 4	Module 5	Module 6	Module 7	Module 8
PIANO LESSONS	Windmill pg. 4	The Bear pg. 5	Arabesque pgs. 6-7	Moving On Up – F Major And D Minor pgs. 8-9 My Own Song – F Major And D Minor pg. 10	Spinning A Yarn pg. 11	Wade In The Water pg. 12	Simple Gifts pg. 13	Innocence pg. 14
THEORY	Two For Six Compound Time pg. 2	Pedaling Has Its Ups And Downs pg. 3	The Score Is Four To One pg. 4 Relay Hand-Off pg. 5	Moving On Up pgs. 6-7 Making A Repeat Appearance! pg. 8	Sixteenth Rests pg. 9 Where Is The Rest Of It? pg. 10		Rhythm Patterns pg. 11	
TECHNIQUE	Full Circle pg. 5 Waterfall pgs. 6, 7 & 8	Elves vs. Giants pgs. 6, 7 & 9	Instant Replay pgs. 10, 11 & 12		Step And Turn pgs. 10, 11 & 13	Rock Bottom pgs. 14, 15 & 16	Alpine Echoes pgs. 14, 15 & 17	Bubble Trail pgs. 18, 19 & 20
SOLOS	The Peppermint Toccata pgs. 3-5	Snowcrystals pgs. 6-7			Starlight Song pgs. 8-9		Sailing pg. 10	

	UNIT 2				UNIT 3			BOOK FIVE
Module 9	Module 10	Module 11	Module 12	Module 13	Module 14	Module 15	Module 16	
A Minor Contribution pg. 15	Cartoon Villain pg. 16	On The Rise pg. 17	Curtain Call pgs. 18-19	The Clown pgs. 20-21	Moving On Up – D Major And B Minor pgs. 22-23 My Own Song – D Major And B Minor pg. 24	A Whispered Promise pg. 25	The Kind Cuckoo pg. 26	PIANO LESSONS
	The Incredible Stretching And Shrinking Chords pg. 12	Chords Of The Key pg. 13 Juggling Triads pgs. 14-15	Season Opener – Major League Triads pg. 16	Treble Clef Steals Third pg. 17	Moving On Up pg. 18 Match Game pg. 19	Questions And Answers pg. 20 Name That Tune! pg. 21	The Dotted Rhythm Website pg. 22	THEORY
Gyroscope pgs. 18, 19 & 21			Wide Open Spaces pgs. 22, 23 & 24			Evening Sky pgs. 22, 23 & 25		TECHNIQUE
On A Grey Day pg. 11			The Great Fountain pgs. 12-13	Crystal Clear pgs. 14-15		Vaudeville Repartée pgs. 16-17		SOLOS

BOOK FIVE	Module 17	Module 18	Module 19	UNIT 4 Module 20	Module 21	Module 22	UNIT 5 Module 23	Module 24
PIANO LESSONS	Nothing Could Be Finer Than Minor pg. 27	Fantasia pg. 28	Scherzino pg. 29	Bouncing Back pg. 30 Michael, Row The Boat Ashore pg. 31	Romance In B Minor pgs. 32-33	Bethena pgs. 34-35	Moving On Up – B♭ Major And G Minor pgs. 36-37 My Own Song – B♭ Major And G Minor pg. 38	Allegro pg. 39
THEORY		Breaking Up Is *Not* Hard To Do pg. 23		Triad Turnovers pgs. 24-25	Inversion Diversion pgs. 26-27		Moving On Up pg. 28 Now Try This! pg. 29	Improvising In A B A Form pg. 30
TECHNIQUE	Soda Pop pgs. 26, 27 & 28	Stepping Stones pgs. 26, 27 & 29		Cookie Cutter 1 pgs. 30, 31 & 32	Cookie Cutter 2 pgs. 30, 31 & 33	Stormy Night pgs. 34, 35 & 36 Second Nature pgs. 34, 35 & 37		
SOLOS	Home Fried Potatoes pgs. 18-19	Song Of The Fisherman pgs. 20-21	Cool Stepper pgs. 22-23	For All The Blessings pgs. 24-26	The Calm Before The Storm pgs. 27-29	Toccatina pgs. 30-31	Prairie School Rag pgs. 32-34	

BOOK FIVE

	Module 25	Module 26	Module 27	UNIT 6 Module 28	Module 29	Module 30	Module 31	Module 32	BOOK FIVE
PIANO LESSONS	Menuet In G Minor pgs. 40-41	Inspector Hound Returns pg. 42	Prelude pg. 43	Gypsy Song pgs. 44-45	Everybody's Blues pg. 46	German Dance pg. 47	Canon In D pgs. 48-50		
THEORY		Chromatic Construction pg. 31; Chromatic Inspection pg. 32	Mysterious Patterns pg. 33	Haven't We Met Before? pgs. 34-35		Thinking It Over pg. 36	Canon In D For Me pg. 37	Spike Is Puzzled pg. 38	
TECHNIQUE	Geometrics pgs. 38, 39 & 40	Dominoes pgs. 38, 39 & 41	Blind Alley pgs. 42, 43 & 44	Even Keel pgs. 42, 43 & 45		Ceremony pgs. 46, 47 & 48			
SOLOS	Nocturne pgs. 35-37	The Bass Man Walketh pgs. 38-39		Remembrances pgs. 40-41	Seagulls pgs. 42-43		Distant Waterfall pgs. 44-47		

The following Improvisation Activities are featured in the *Imagine & Create* sections of *Piano Practice Games Book 2.*

Piano Practice Games present imaginative ways to introduce pieces in **Piano Lessons** by coordinating technique, concepts, and creativity with the actual music in the lesson book. These preparation activities help focus learning by "playing with" each lesson piece aurally, visually, and physically.

Before each lesson piece is assigned:

Listen & Respond activities develop rhythmic and technical coordination.

active listening

Read & Discover activities reinforce understanding and recognition of musical patterns and symbols.

guided reading

After each lesson piece is mastered:

Imagine & Create activities expand knowledge of newly-learned concepts.

improvising and composing

Whether used in private or group lessons, **Piano Games** are all designed to make music. Many activities include accompaniments that can be added in the following ways:

Teacher

Audio CD

General MIDI Disk

Imagine & Create

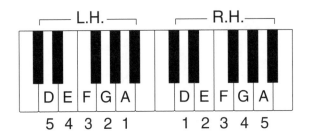

Change the mood of *Andantino!*

1. Place your hands in this position two octaves above middle C.
    Note that this is one key higher than the *Andantino* position.

2. As your teacher plays the accompaniment below, play *Andantino* in
    this new position. Use the same finger numbers and keep the shape
    and rhythm of the melody the same.

Teacher Accompaniment

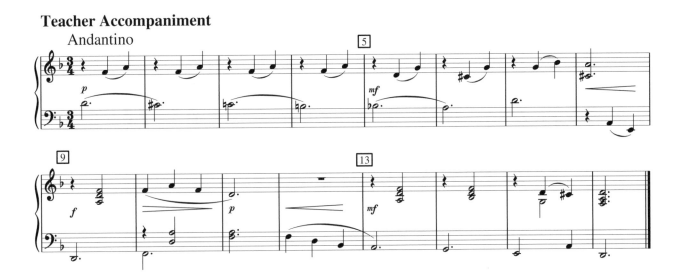

Imagine & Create

Get ready to improvise!

Place your hands in the *Travelling Along The Prairie* position and get ready to improvise a new piece titled *Orange Horizon*.

1. Practice playing this repeated accompaniment (ostinato) with your L.H.

Repeat as necessary

2. After you can play the accompaniment easily, improvise a R.H. melody with the notes D E G A. Try playing your melody one octave higher.

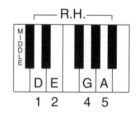

Orange Horizon

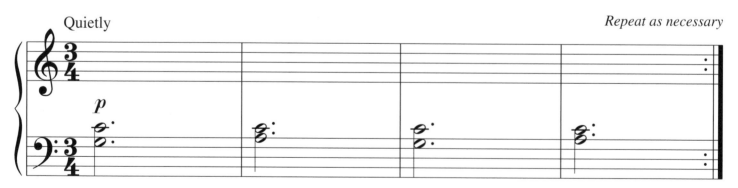

Quietly

Repeat as necessary

Hold damper pedal down throughout.

3. When you are ready to end your piece, rest your R.H. and let the L.H. accompaniment continue. Gradually fade away by playing softer and softer, slower and slower.

Imagine & Create

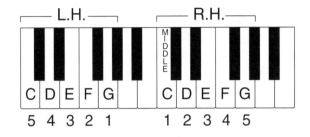

All that's missing is you!

Place your hands in the *Watercolors* hand position. As you listen to *Watercolors*, make up your own melody using the notes C D E F G in the empty measures. Play in the rhythm shown.

Imagine & Create

Let your hands talk to each other!

One way to create a piece is to trade phrases between your hands, playing first one hand and then the other. Make up your own piece using the following notes in both hands:

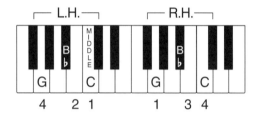

1. As you listen to the accompaniment to *A Little Latin*, play along as your R.H. asks a musical question and your L.H. answers back.

2. As your teacher plays the 12-bar blues accompaniment below, make up your own melody using the same notes in question and answer phrases between the hands.

Teacher Accompaniment
   Moderately fast ($\quad$ = 170)

Imagine & Create

Get ready to improvise!

1. In jazz style, a repeated accompaniment pattern is called a **vamp**. Practice playing the L.H. vamp below.

Repeat as necessary

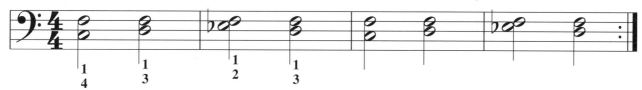

2. When you can play the L.H. vamp easily, use it as an introduction to your improvisation. Keep the vamp going as you improvise a melody in your R.H. using notes C D E♭ F.

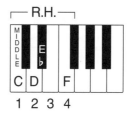

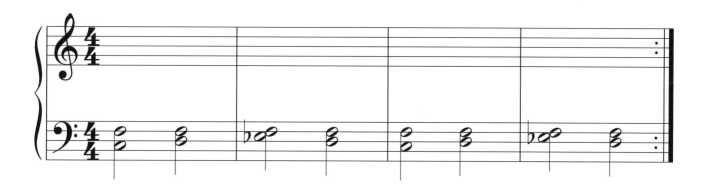

3. When you are ready to complete your improvisation, add the following ending:

Pop!

(Lesson Book 2, pg. 43)

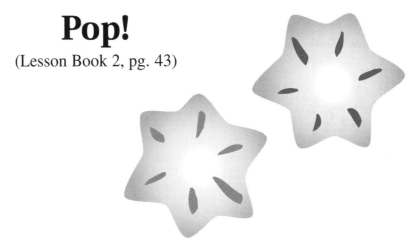

Create a new piece in A B A form!

1. As you listen to the accompaniment to *My Own Song on G A B C D*, play *Pop!* from your lesson book one octave higher than written. This is the A section of your piece.

2. Using the notes G A B C D, make up your own B section by improvising for eight or more measures.

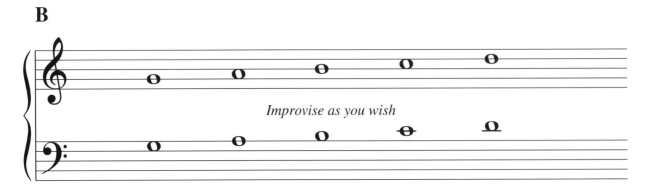

3. Return to the beginning of *Pop!* (in jazz, that's called the "head") and play to the end of the piece.

Hal Leonard Student Piano Library
Authors

Barbara Kreader, Method Author	Fred Kern, Method Author, Series Arranger/Composer	Phillip Keveren, Method Author, Series Arranger/Composer	Mona Rejino, Method Author, Series Arranger/Composer	Karen Harrington, *Notespeller* Author, *Theory* Books Co-Author

BARBARA KREADER has given workshops throughout the United States, Canada, New Zealand, Australia, Asia, and the United Kingdom. She maintains a private studio in Evanston, Illinois, where she teaches 45 students. Ms. Kreader is the editor for the Parent/Teacher/Child department of *Keyboard Companion* and is a frequent contributor to *Clavier* magazine. In the summer months, she is Program Director for the Junior Student Seminars at Rocky Ridge Music Center in Estes Park, Colorado. Ms. Kreader holds a M.M. in piano performance from Northwestern University.

FRED KERN is Professor of Music and a specialist in piano education at the University of North Texas in Denton where he is Coordinator of Keyboard Skills and Music Fundamentals. Widely known as a clinician, author, teacher, composer and arranger, he has published five texts and two methods on piano instruction. Dr. Kern holds graduate degrees in piano performance, music education, and piano pedagogy from Illinois Wesleyan, Northwestern University, and the University of Northern Colorado. He is certified as a Master Teacher through MTNA.

PHILLIP KEVEREN, a multi-talented keyboard artist and composer, has composed original works in a variety of genres from piano solo to symphonic orchestra. His original piano collections include *New Piano Impressions* and *Presto Scherzo,* and his popular arrangements are featured in *The Phillip Keveren Series.* Mr. Keveren gives over 50 concerts and workshops yearly in the United States, Canada, Europe and Asia. He is a contributing composer to the *Hal Leonard Showcase Solos Series*, and creates all the orchestrated CD/General MIDI accompaniments for the *Hal Leonard Student Piano Library.*

MONA REJINO, an accomplished pianist, teacher, and composer, has maintained an independent piano studio in Carrollton, Texas from 1983 to the present. She is an active adjudicator and performer in the Dallas area and teaches at The Hockaday School. Ms. Rejino has conducted numerous workshops across the United States, and is a contributing composer to the *Hal Leonard Showcase Solos Series.* Ms. Rejino holds a Bachelor of Music degree from West Texas State University, and a M.M. degree in piano performance from The University of North Texas where she studied with Joseph Banowetz.

KAREN HARRINGTON is an independent piano teacher from Tulsa, Oklahoma where she maintains a studio of more than forty students. She has taught piano for over nineteen years, and is active as an adjudicator and clinician as well. A nationally certified teacher through MTNA, she is a past president of both the *Tulsa Accredited Music Teachers Association* and the *Northeast District of Oklahoma Music Teachers Association.* Karen has also served as Secretary and President of the *South Central Division* of MTNA. She holds a BME degree from the University of Oklahoma where she studied piano with Celia Mae Bryant. Ms. Harrington produces her own theory games through her company, *Music Games 'N Things.*

Peggy Otwell,
Director of Educational
Keyboard Publications

DR. PEGGY OTWELL brings an impressive combination of performing and teaching experience to her role as *Director of Educational Keyboard Publications* at Hal Leonard. She began teaching during her undergraduate studies at Catholic University in Washington, DC, and has maintained an independent piano studio for over twenty-five years. An active member of MTNA since 1978, she is a past president of the *Northern Virginia Music Teachers Association.* Peggy has served on faculties of the University of Maryland Eastern Shore, American University Preparatory Department, and George Mason University. She has given lecture-recitals, workshops and master classes, and has appeared in solo and chamber music performances throughout the USA and in Europe. Peggy was awarded a DMA degree in piano performance from the University of Maryland, where she studied piano and pedagogy with renowned teachers Stewart Gordon, Thomas Schumacher, and Nelita True.

From the very first lessons in **Book 1**, students are making music as they explore the piano keyboard through fun improvisation pieces called *My Own Song*. The beginning of the book introduces finger numbers, the black-key and white-key groups, and basic rhythm patterns.

Directional reading is taught first by finger number, then by note name, and then by interval (step, skip, and repeat). Once the students are introduced to the staff, they learn reading guides **Bass F** and **Treble G** and read by interval in several different hand positions.

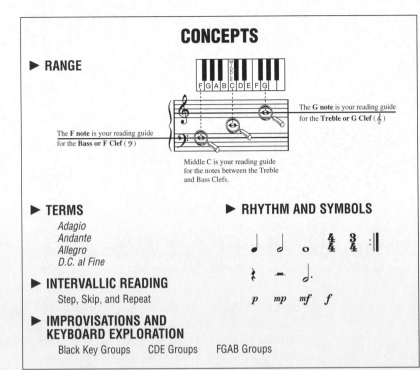

CONCEPTS

► **RANGE**

The **F note** is your reading guide for the **Bass or F Clef** (𝄢)

The **G note** is your reading guide for the **Treble or G Clef** (𝄞)

Middle C is your reading guide for the notes between the Treble and Bass Clefs.

► **TERMS**
Adagio
Andante
Allegro
D.C. al Fine

► **INTERVALLIC READING**
Step, Skip, and Repeat

► **IMPROVISATIONS AND KEYBOARD EXPLORATION**
Black Key Groups   CDE Groups   FGAB Groups

► **RHYTHM AND SYMBOLS**

PRACTICE and PERFORMANCE tempos included on each CD!

SERIES BOOKS THAT CORRELATE PAGE-BY-PAGE WITH *PIANO LESSONS BOOK 1*

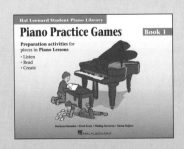

Book 2 opens with a new *My Own Song* improvisation on CDEFG. Unit 1 introduces phrasing and legato touch, and also presents harmonic 2nds and 3rds with staccato touch. The following two units are dedicated to the introduction of 4ths and 5ths.

Also in Unit 3, sharps are introduced in a diatonic setting starting on D, and flats are introduced as blues notes. Most pieces in the second half of **Book 2** coordinate hands playing together.

This book works very well for transfer students.

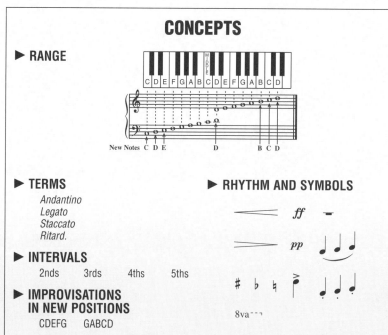

CONCEPTS

▶ **RANGE**

New Notes C D E   D   B C D

▶ **TERMS**
Andantino
Legato
Staccato
Ritard.

▶ **INTERVALS**
2nds   3rds   4ths   5ths

▶ **IMPROVISATIONS IN NEW POSITIONS**
CDEFG   GABCD

▶ **RHYTHM AND SYMBOLS**

ff   *pp*

♭ ♮

8va⁻⁻⁻

Big Ben

PRACTICE and PERFORMANCE tempos included on each CD!

Brass Fanfare

SERIES BOOKS THAT CORRELATE PAGE-BY-PAGE WITH *PIANO LESSONS BOOK 2*

Unit 1 of **Book 3** opens with eighth notes first in 4/4 time, then in 2/4 time. Swing eighths are also presented in the first half of the book. Folk, jazz, classical, and contemporary selections provide students with an interesting variety of repertoire.

In the second half of **Book 3**, five-finger patterns and triads in C Major, G Major, and F Major are presented, as well as their relative minors – A Minor, E Minor, and D Minor.

CONCEPTS

▶ **RANGE**

▶ **TERMS**
Loco
A tempo
D.S. al Fine
D.C. al Coda

▶ **INTERVALS**
6ths   half-steps   whole-steps

▶ **FIVE-FINGER PATTERNS**
C Major   G Major   F Major
A Minor   E Minor   D Minor

▶ **FIVE-FINGER PATTERN IMPROVISATIONS**
using the six patterns listed here

▶ **RHYTHM AND SYMBOLS**

2/4

15ma- - -

PRACTICE and PERFORMANCE tempos included on each CD!

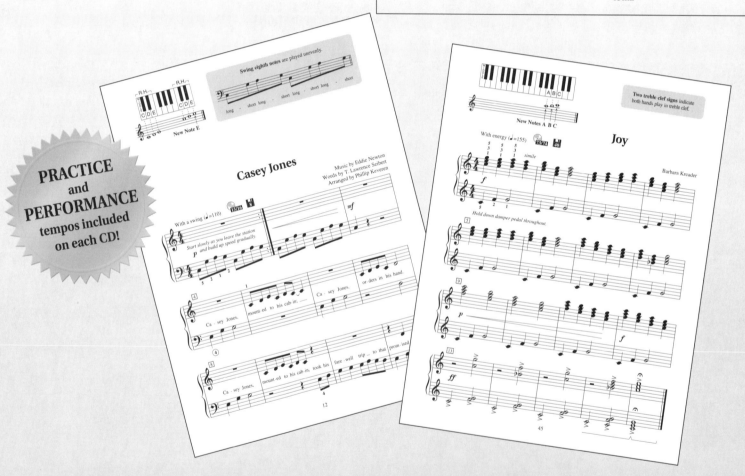

SERIES BOOKS THAT CORRELATE PAGE-BY-PAGE WITH *PIANO LESSONS BOOK 3*

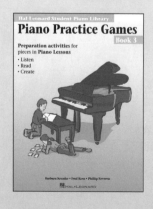

Book 4 expands on the related five-finger patterns learned in Book 3 to introduce the scales of C Major, A Minor, G Major, and E Minor. Chord progressions in close position are also presented in each of these keys.

Syncopated rhythms, syncopated pedaling and opposing articulations between the hands create performances with style, color, and texture.

CONCEPTS

▶ **RANGE**

▶ **TERMS**

Allegretto	*Con moto*
Moderato	*Giocoso*
Poco	*Presto*
Vivace	

▶ **INTERVALS**

7ths   8ths (octave)

▶ **SCALES AND CHORD PROGRESSIONS**

C Major   G Major
A Minor   E Minor

▶ **PRIMARY TRIADS**

Tonic   Sub-dominant   Dominant

▶ **RELATED KEY IMPROVISATIONS**

Combining C Major with A Minor
Combining G Major with E Minor

▶ **RHYTHM AND SYMBOLS**

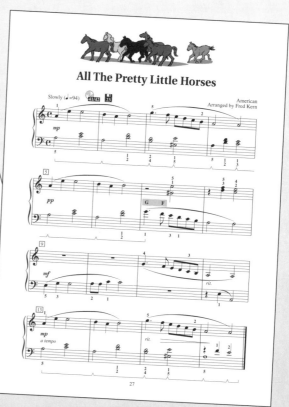

PRACTICE and PERFORMANCE tempos included on each CD!

SERIES BOOKS THAT CORRELATE PAGE-BY-PAGE WITH *PIANO LESSONS BOOK 4*

In **Book 5**, students are introduced to sixteenth notes in various rhythm patterns. The wide variety of student selections include 3 folk, 4 jazz, 13 classical, and 8 contemporary original pieces.

Scales (in both 8th and 16th-note patterns) with their cadences are presented in five major and five minor keys. Root, 1st inversion, 2nd inversion, and open position chords for each key center are also introduced.

CONCEPTS

▶ **TERMS**

Accelerando	Allargando
Dolce	Espressivo
Grazioso	Leggiero
Marcato	Molto
Morendo	Pesante
Portato	Portamento
Scherzando	Sforzando sfz
Subito	Tempo primo

▶ **RHYTHM AND SYMBOLS**

▶ **SCALES WITH I-IV-I AND I-V-V7-I CADENCES**

C Major	G Major	F Major	D Major	B♭ Major
A Minor	E Minor	D Minor	B Minor	G Minor
Chromatic Scales				

▶ **PRIMARY AND SECONDARY TRIADS**

Root Position, 1st Inversion, 2nd Inversion, Open Position

▶ **CHORD QUALITIES**

Major   Minor   Diminished   Augmented

▶ **RELATED KEY IMPROVISATIONS**

- Developing Motives and Sequences
- Creating Question and Answer Phrases
- Using ABA Form

PRACTICE and PERFORMANCE tempos included on each CD!

SERIES BOOKS THAT CORRELATE PAGE-BY-PAGE WITH *PIANO LESSONS BOOK 5*

Index of Supplementary Materials

Technique Classics
Pgs. 80-81

Popular Piano Solos
Pg. 82

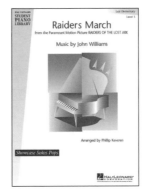

Showcase Solos Pops
Pg. 83

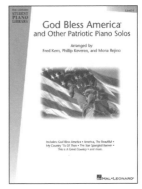

Patriotic Solos
Pg. 84

Patriotic Duets
Pg. 84

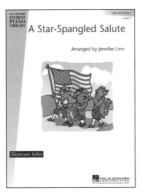

Patriotic Sheet Music
Pg. 84

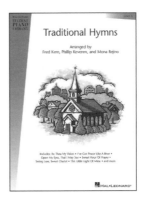

Traditional Hymns
Pg. 85

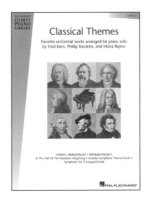

Classical Themes
Pg. 85

Christmas Piano Solos
Pg. 86

Seasonal Jewish Songbooks
Pg. 86

Piano Ensembles
Pg. 87

Showcase Solos
Pgs. 88-89

Composer Showcase
Pg. 90

The Phillip Keveren Series
Pg. 91

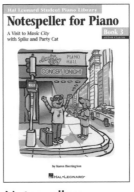

Notespellers
Pg. 92

Other Teaching Aids
Pg. 92

Technique Classics

Hanon for the Developing Pianist

*Drawing on the original G. Schirmer edition, this new G. Schirmer edition in the **Hal Leonard Student Piano Library** was created with today's developing pianist in mind.*

This fresh look at Hanon's popular studies includes:

- Innovative student worksheets
- Orchestrated CD and GM accompaniments by Phillip Keveren
- Informative historical and biographical facts
- Chromatic-scale exercises

We invite you to rediscover Hanon's classic exercises in this exciting new edition!

Download a complimentary *Virtuoso Variations* chart for these Hanon exercises at our website today!
http://www.halleonard.com/pianoed.jsp

Also available:

Hanon for the Developing Pianist
00296165 Book/CD
00296183 Book Only
00296184 GM Disk Only

Technique Classics

Czerny Selections from The Little Pianist, Opus 823

The second book in the Technique Classics series features a collection of little-known early-intermediate level etudes by Carl Czerny. Drawn from the original G. Schirmer edition, this new edition is a must for every studio.

Available in Book/CD Package!

This new edition of Czerny's classic etudes includes:

- 29 etudes in original form for the early-intermediate student
- Innovative student worksheets
- Orchestrated CD and GM disk accompaniments by Phillip Keveren
- Informative biographical and historical facts

Czerny Selections from The Little Pianist, Opus 823
00296363   Book/CD
00296364   Book Only
00296365   GM Disk Only

Also available:

Popular Piano Solos

Songs students know and love with great teacher accompaniments!
Instrumental accompaniments are also available on CD and GM disk.
Arranged by Bill Boyd, Fred Kern, Phillip Keveren, Mona Rejino, Robert Vandall, and Carol Klose.

Popular Piano Solos

Level 1
7 songs w/ teacher accompaniments: Baby Bumblebee • It's A Small World • The Siamese Cat Song • John Jacob Jingleheimer Schmidt • Jingle Jangle Jingle (I Got Spurs) • The Marvelous Toy • Let's Go Fly A Kite.

00296031   Book Only
00296093   CD Only
00296094   GM Disk Only

Level 2
11 songs w/ teacher accompaniments: Alley Cat Song • Be Our Guest • Can You Feel The Love Tonight? • Chopsticks • Do-Re-Mi • Edelweiss • Give My Regards To Broadway • Happy Days • I'm Popeye The Sailor Man • Somewhere Out There • Supercalafragilisticexpialidocious.

00296032   Book Only
00296095   CD Only
00296096   GM Disk Only

Level 3
9 songs, w/ some teacher accompaniments: At The Hop • Baby Elephant Walk • Beauty And The Beast • Chim Chim Cher-ee • The Glory Of Love • In The Mood • The Munster's Theme • Raiders March • Yellow Submarine.

00296033   Book Only
00296097   CD Only
00296098   GM Disk Only

Level 4
7 songs: Cruella De Vil • Theme From E.T. (The Extra-Terrestrial) • Forrest Gump – Main Title (Feather Theme) • The Muppet Show Theme • My Favorite Things • The Rainbow Connection • Under The Sea.

00296053   Book Only
00296099   CD Only
00296100   GM Disk Only

Level 5
12 songs: Can You Feel The Love Tonight • Candle On The Water • Castle On A Cloud • Chariots Of Fire • Hey Jude • Mission: Impossible Theme • My Heart Will Go On (Love Theme from 'Titanic') • Star Trek – The Next Generation® • You'll Be In My Heart • You've Got A Friend In Me • Ob-La-Di, Ob-La-Da • Y.M.C.A.

00296147   Book Only
00296157   CD Only
00296158   GM Disk Only

More Popular Piano Solos

Level 1
7 songs w/ teacher accompaniments: The Bells of Notre Dame • 'C' Is For Cookie • Circle Of Life • Feed The Birds • Mickey Mouse March • On Top Of Spaghetti • Winnie The Pooh.

00296189   Book Only
00296260   CD Only
00296263   GM Disk Only

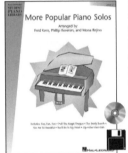

Level 2
11 songs w/ teacher accompaniments: Bella Notte • The Brady Bunch • Fun, Fun, Fun • My Heart Will Go On (Love Theme From 'Titanic') • Puff The Magic Dragon • Raindrops Keep Fallin' On My Head • Sing • Y.M.C.A. • You Are So Beautiful • You'll Be In My Heart • Zip-A-Dee-Doo-Dah.

00296190   Book Only
00296261   CD Only
00296264   GM Disk Only

Level 3
12 songs, some w/ teacher accompaniments: The Bare Necessities • Climb Ev'ry Mountain • A Dream Is A Wish Your Heart Makes • Go The Distance • God Help The Outcasts • I Whistle A Happy Tune • Once Upon A Dream • Part Of Your World • Sesame Street Theme • Stand By Me • Tomorrow • What A Wonderful World.

00296191   Book Only
00296262   CD Only
00296265   GM Disk Only

Level 4
12 songs: Fields Of Gold • Kiss The Girl • Let It Be • Memory • My Funny Valentine • On Broadway • The Phantom Of The Opera • Rainy Days And Mondays • Reflection • Unchained Melody • A Whole New World • When I'm Sixty-Four.

00296192   Book Only
00296274   CD Only
00296265   GM Disk Only

Level 5
14 songs: All I Ask Of You • Be Our Guest • Colors Of The Wind • From A Distance • Hero • I Dreamed A Dream • I Want To Spend My Lifetime Loving You • I Will Remember You • Imagine • Linus And Lucy • The Sound Of Music • Southampton • Take Five • There You'll Be.

00296193   Book Only
00296275   CD Only
00296277   GM Disk Only

Showcase Solos Pops

Showcase Solos Pops is a graded series featuring sheet music arrangements of movie themes, Broadway classics, favorite children's songs, and today's top recorded hits. Each solo is expertly arranged with a winning combination of creativity and solid pedagogy. These exciting pieces for beginners through intermediate level students provide excellent supplementary material for any method, and are a perfect complement to the **Hal Leonard Student Piano Library**.

"C" Is For Cookie *(Phillip Keveren)*
00296267 Early Elementary (Level 1)

Cruella De Vil *(Mona Rejino)*
00296270 Early Intermediate (Level 4)

Mission: Impossible Theme *(Fred Kern)*
00296272 Intermediate (Level 5)

Raiders March *(Phillip Keveren)*
00296269 Late Elementary (Level 3)

Sing *(Fred Kern)*
00296268 Elementary (Level 2)

A Spoonful Of Sugar *(Mona Rejino)*
00296271 Early Intermediate (Level 4)

Winnie The Pooh *(Fred Kern)*
00296266 Early Elementary (Level 1)

Y.M.C.A. *(Fred Kern)*
00296273 Intermediate (Level 5)

Patriotic Piano Music

God Bless America® and Other Patriotic Piano Solos

Arranged by Fred Kern, Phillip Keveren and Mona Rejino, each book contains an arrangement of "God Bless America" and many other favorite American patriotic melodies, many with great teacher accompaniments.

Level 1
7 songs: Battle Hymn Of The Republic • God Bless America • God Bless Our Native Land • I Believe • If I Had A Hammer (The Hammer Song) • This Land Is Your Land • We Shall Overcome.
00296249

Level 2
8 songs: America, The Beautiful • God Bless America • Let There Be Peace On Earth • My Country, 'Tis Of Thee (America) • The Star Spangled Banner • This Is A Great Country • This Is My Country • You're A Grand Old Flag.
00296250

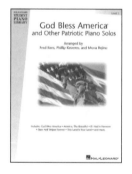

Level 3
8 solos: America, The Beautiful • God Bless America • God Bless Our Native Land • I Believe • If I Had A Hammer (The Hammer Song) • Stars And Stripes Forever • This Land Is Your Land • We Shall Overcome.
00296255

Level 4
8 solos: America, The Beautiful • God Bless America • Let There Be Peace On Earth • My Country, 'Tis Of Thee (America) • The Star Spangled Banner • This Is A Great Country • This Is My Country • You're A Grand Old Flag.
00296256

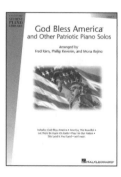

Level 5
8 solos: America, The Beautiful • Battle Hymn Of The Republic • God Bless America • Let There Be Peace On Earth • Pray For Our Nation • Stars And Stripes Forever • This Land Is Your Land •We Shall Overcome.
00296257

God Bless America® – Patriotic Duets for Piano

For Levels 3, 4, and 5. Each book features equal-part duet arrangements of classic American patriotic songs, arranged by favorite HLSPL composers for one piano, four hands.

Level 3
6 duets: America, The Beautiful • God Bless America • Let There Be Peace On Earth • My Country, 'Tis Of Thee (America) • Stars And Stripes Forever • You're A Grand Old Flag.
00296251

Level 4
6 duets: America, The Beautiful • Battle Hymn Of The Republic • God Bless America • My Country, 'Tis Of Thee (America) • The Star Spangled Banner • This Is My Country.
00296252

Level 5
6 Duets: America, The Beautiful • Battle Hymn Of The Republic • God Bless America • The Star Spangled Banner • Stars And Stripes Forever • You're A Grand Old Flag.
00296253

Patriotic Sheet Music

Presenting 12 exciting patriotic solos in the *Showcase Solos* series! Arranged by your favorite **Hal Leonard Student Piano Library** composers, these up-lifting songs celebrating the spirit of America are sure to be a hit with all your students.

Early Elementary (Level 1)	
00296238	God Bless America (Berlin/arr. Mona Rejino)
00296243	My Country, 'Tis Of Thee (America) (arr. Carol Klose)

Elementary (Level 2)	
00296244	America, The Beautiful (arr. Mona Rejino)
00296239	God Bless America (Berlin/arr. Carol Klose)

Late Elementary (Level 3)	
00296240	God Bless America (Berlin/arr. Jennifer Linn)
00296245	A Star-Spangled Salute (arr. Jennifer Linn)
00296254	This Is A Great Country (Berlin/arr. Barrett Byers)

Early Intermediate (Level 4)	
00296241	God Bless America (Berlin/arr. Fred Kern)
00296246	This Is My Country (arr. Matthew Edwards)

Intermediate (Level 5)	
00296248	America, The Beautiful (arr. Christos Tsitsaros)
00296247	Battle Hymn of the Republic (arr. Fred Kern)
00296242	God Bless America (Berlin/arr. Phillip Keveren)

Traditional Hymns

Favorite traditional hymns, carefully graded and arranged for piano with great teacher accompaniments! Instrumental accompaniments are also available on CD and GM disk. Arranged by Fred Kern, Phillip Keveren, and Mona Rejino. Available in five levels: Early Elementary to Intermediate piano solos.

Level 1
7 songs: Amazing Grace • Deep And Wide • Faith Of Our Fathers • For The Beauty Of The Earth • Give Me That Old Time Religion • Jesus Loves Me • Praise God, From Whom All Blessings Flow.

00296196 Book Only
00296278 CD Only
00296283 GM Disk Only

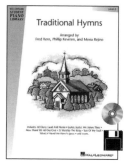

Level 2
11 songs: All Glory, Laud And Honor • Be Still, My Soul • Come, Christians, Join To Sing • Down In My Heart • I Sing The Mighty Power Of God • Joyful, Joyful, We Adore Thee • Now Thank We All Our God • O Worship The King • Praise Him, All Ye Little Children • Sun Of My Soul • What A Friend We Have In Jesus.

00296198 Book Only
00296279 CD Only
00296284 GM Disk Only

Level 3
14 songs: All Things Bright And Beautiful • Come, Thou Almighty King • Dear Lord And Father Of Mankind • Ezekiel Saw The Wheel • From All That Dwell Below The Skies • God Of Grace And God Of Glory • Holy, Holy, Holy! Lord God Almighty • It Is Well With My Soul • Jacob's Ladder • Lead On, O King Eternal • Little David Play On Your Harp • A Mighty Fortress Is Our God • Tell Me The Stories Of Jesus • Zacchaeus.

00296197 Book Only
00296280 CD Only
00296285 GM Disk Only

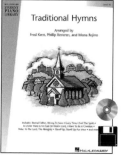

Level 4
12 songs: Eternal Father, Strong To Save • Every Time I Feel The Spirit • God Will Take Care Of You • In Christ There Is No East Or West • Lord, I Want To Be A Christian • My Faith Looks Up To Thee • Nobody Knows The Trouble I've Seen • Once To Every Man And Nation • Praise To The Lord, The Almighty • Softly And Tenderly • Stand Up, Stand Up For Jesus • This Is My Father's World.

00296199 Book Only
00296281 CD Only
00296286 GM Disk Only

Level 5
14 songs: Be Thou My Vision • Blessed Assurance • Church In The Wildwood • Give Me Oil In My Lamp • I've Got Peace Like A River • In The Garden • Jesus Loves Even Me (I Am So Glad) • Let The Lower Lights Be Burning • Open My Eyes, That I May See • Rejoice, The Lord Is King • Savior, Like A Shepherd Lead Us • Sweet Hour Of Prayer • Swing Low, Sweet Chariot • This Little Light Of Mine.

00296200 Book Only
00296282 CD Only
00296287 GM Disk Only

Classical Themes
for Piano Solo

Favorite orchestral classics, carefully graded and arranged for piano solo with great teacher accompaniments! Instrumental accompaniments are also available on CD and GM disk. Arranged by Fred Kern, Phillip Keveren and Mona Rejino.

Level 1
8 orchestral classics: Air • Can-Can • The Emperor Waltz • Morning • Russian Dance ("Trepak") • Theme From Swan Lake • Symphony No. 3 ("Eroica") • Trumpet Voluntary.

00296323 Book Only
00296328 CD Only
00296333 GM Disk Only

Level 2
10 orchestral classics: Alleluia • Barcarolle • Eine Kleine Nachtmusik ("Romanze") • Hallelujah • In The Hall Of The Mountain King • Largo From Symphony No. 9 ("New World") • March Militaire, Op. 51, No. 1 • Plaisir d'amour • The Sleeping Beauty Waltz • The Surprise Symphony.

00296324 Book Only
00296329 CD Only
00296334 GM Disk Only

Level 3
10 orchestral classics: The Elephant • La donna è mobile • Lullaby (Cradle Song) • Merry Widow Waltz • Polovetsian Dance • Rosamunde • Scheherazade • Symphony No. 1, First Movement • Trumpet Tune • Turkish March.

00296325 Book Only
00296330 CD Only
00296335 GM Disk Only

Level 4
10 orchestral classics: Ave Maria • 1812 Overture • Funeral March Of A Marionette • O mio babbino caro • Overture To Carmen • Pilgrims' Chorus • Rondeau • Symphony No. 6 ("Pathetique") • Symphony No. 7, Second Movement • Symphony No. 9 ("From The New World").

00296326 Book Only
00296331 CD Only
00296336 GM Disk Only

Level 5
10 orchestral classics: Air On The G String • Also Sprach Zarathustra, Opening Theme • Finale • Hungarian Dance No. 5 • Jesu, Joy Of Man's Desiring • Romeo And Juliet (Love Theme) • Sicilienne • Spring • Symphony No. 40, First Movement • William Tell Overture.

00296327 Book Only
00296332 CD Only
00296337 GM Disk Only

Seasonal Songbooks

Favorite carols and seasonal songs, many with great teacher accompaniments!
Instrumental accompaniments are also available on CD and GM disk.
Arranged by Fred Kern, Phillip Keveren, Mona Rejino, and Bruce Berr.

Christmas Piano Solos

Level 1

7 songs w/ teacher accompaniments: Away In A Manger • Go Tell It On The Mountain • Good King Wenceslas • Jingle Bells • Jolly Old Saint Nicholas • O Come, O Come Immanuel • We Three Kings Of Orient Are.

00296049   Book Only
00296081   CD Only
00296101   GM Disk Only

Level 4

13 songs: Angels We Have Heard On High • The Christmas Song • Feliz Navidad • Hark! The Herald Angels Sing • The Holly And The Ivy • A Holly Jolly Christmas • (There's No Place Like) Home For The Holidays • It's Beginning To Look Like Christmas • Jingle-Bell Rock • Joy To The World • March Of The Toys • Parade Of The Wooden Soldiers • Silver Bells.

00296052   Book Only
00296084   CD Only
00296104   GM Disk Only

Level 2

11 songs w/ teacher accompaniments: God Rest Ye Merry, Gentlemen • I Saw Three Ships • It Came Upon The Midnight Clear • Joseph Dearest, Joseph Mine • O Come, All Ye Faithful • O Come, Little Children • O Little Town Of Bethleham • Silent Night • Sing We Now Of Christmas • Up On The Housetop • What Child Is This?

00296050   Book Only
00296082   CD Only
00296102   GM Disk Only

Level 5

12 songs: The Christmas Waltz • Dance Of The Sugar Plum Fairy • God Rest Ye Merry, Gentlemen • I Wonder As I Wander • Jingle Bell Classic • Let It Snow! Let It Snow! Let It Snow! • March from "The Nutcracker Ballet Suite" • Mary Had A Baby • Mister Santa • Still, Still, Still • Tennessee Christmas • Toyland.

00296146   Book Only
00296159   CD Only
00296162   GM Disk Only

Level 3

11 songs, some w/ teacher accompaniments: Carol Of The Bells • The Chipmunk Song • Deck The Hall • The First Noel • Frosty The Snow Man • My Favorite Things • O Christmas Tree • Rockin' Around The Christmas Tree • Rudolph The Red-Nosed Reindeer • We Need A Little Christmas • We Wish You A Merry Christmas.

00296051   Book Only
00296083   CD Only
00296103   GM Disk Only

Seasonal Jewish Songbooks

Festive Chanukah Songs Level 2

Arranged by Bruce Berr

7 songs: Candle Blessings • Chanukah • Come Light The Menorah • Hanérot, Halalu • The Dreydl Song • S'vivon • Ma'oz Tsur.

00296194

Festive Songs for the Jewish Holidays Level 3

Arranged by Bruce Berr

11 songs: Who Can Retell? • Come Light The Menorah • S'Vivon • Ma'oz Tsur • I Have A Little Dreydl • Dayénu • Ma Nishtana • Adir Hu • Eliyahu Hanavi • Chad Gadya • Hatikvah.

00296195

Piano Ensembles

Four-part student ensembles arranged for two or more pianos.
Instrumental accompaniments are also available on CD and GM disk.
These ensembles, arranged by Phillip Keveren, feature student favorites
from *Piano Lessons* books 1-5 of the **Hal Leonard Student Piano Library**.

Level 1
Night Shadows • Party Cat • Trumpet Man •
Go For The Gold.

00296064   Book Only
00296073   CD Only
00296074   GM Disk Only

Level 2
Painted Rocking Horse • Basketball Bounce •
Stompin' • Summer Evenings.

00296065   Book Only
00296075   CD Only
00296076   GM Disk Only

Level 3
Dixieland Jam • Scherzo • Street Fair • Fresh Start.

00296066   Book Only
00296077   CD Only
00296078   GM Disk Only

Level 4
Carpet Ride • Calypso Cat • Jig • Allegro
from Eine Kleine Nachtmusik.

00296067   Book Only
00296079   CD Only
00296080   GM Disk Only

Level 5
Wade In The Water • A Minor Contribution •
A Whispered Promise • Gypsy Song.

00296090   Book Only
00296091   CD Only
00296092   GM Disk Only

Each book of the *Piano Ensembles*
series contains four favorite selections
from the corresponding *Piano Lessons*
book and includes:

- Four student parts
- Conductor's score with optional
  teacher accompaniment
- Performance configurations
  for 2 or more pianos
- Suggested instrumentation
  for electronic keyboard

from Piano Ensembles Level 1

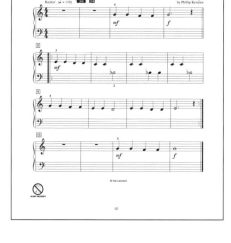

Hal Leonard Student Piano Library
Showcase Solos Composers

Rosemary Barrett Byers

ROSEMARY BARRETT BYERS has enjoyed a varied career as pianist, conductor, theatrical director, teacher, composer, and arranger. Since completing a Master of Music degree in piano performance at Indiana University, she has taught children and adults of all ages and levels in a home studio and at various colleges and universities throughout the Southeast and Midwest. Several of her original children's musicals, including *CinderElf*, and *The Weally Weird Wabbitt* have been produced by theater companies in Tennessee and Kentucky. Other published piano compositions include *Cat Tales*, *More Cat Tales*, *Clown-U-Copia*, and *Blues Suite.*

Bruce Berr

BRUCE BERR has been teaching music to children and adults for over thirty years. He has taught piano and piano pedagogy in a variety of settings: universities and colleges, community music schools, and in his home studio. Dr. Berr has written extensively about the art of teaching piano. He has been an associate editor and webmaster for *Keyboard Companion* magazine since 1997. He has presented lectures and workshops for professional music teachers' associations and conventions throughout the United States. He is currently Chair of the Composition Competition for the *National Conference on Keyboard Pedagogy*. Dr. Berr received his degrees in piano and pedagogy from Washington University in St. Louis and from Northwestern University.

Bill Boyd

BILL BOYD (1933-2001) played piano professionally as both a solo performer and band member in hotels, supper clubs, and private clubs in New York and Long Island. Mr. Boyd composed numerous jazz collections including the *Think Jazz* piano method and the *Jazz Starters* series for beginners. Mr. Boyd was awarded a Master's degree from Columbia University and taught junior high school band and stage band in Huntington, Long Island for over 20 years. After retiring from teaching, Mr. Boyd devoted all his time to arranging and composing.

Sondra Clark

SONDRA CLARK is a graduate of The Juilliard School of Music in New York City, San Jose State University, and Stanford University, where she completed her Ph.D. Her composition teachers have included Vincent Persichetti, Norman Lloyd, and George Perle. Dr. Clark was a member of the San Jose State University Music Faculty for twelve years. She is an internationally recognized specialist on the music of Charles Ives and a long-time Bay Area music critic. Dr. Clark now devotes herself to composing full time, and since 1990, over forty of her compositions have won awards, one of which was a 2001 ASCAP award.

Matthew Edwards

MATTHEW EDWARDS studied piano with Laurence Morton and Robert Weirich, and in 1999, he completed his Doctor of Musical Arts degree in piano performance at the Peabody Conservatory of Music, under the instruction of Robert McDonald. Currently, he is a member of the music faculties at Anne Arundel Community College, Howard Community College, and Washington Bible College. Additionally, Matthew serves as the Director of Music and Youth at the Harvester Baptist Church in Columbia, Maryland, and maintains a private piano studio at his home.

Carol Klose

CAROL KLOSE, an accomplished pianist, teacher, and composer, holds piano performance degrees from Rosary College and Villa Schifanoia Graduate School of Fine Arts, Italy. Formerly on the faculty of the Wisconsin College/Conservatory of Music, Milwaukee, she teaches piano privately and is a frequent adjudicator and clinician. Additional published works include original compositions in the new NGPT Allison Contemporary Piano Collection, as well as numerous solos, duets, and folios arranged for students.

Jennifer Linn

JENNIFER LINN, an accomplished performer and composer in St. Louis, Missouri, has maintained a private studio for over 17 years. Her compositions have been selected for the National Federation of Music Clubs' festival list and have been featured in *Keys* magazine. In 1999-2000, Ms. Linn served as Visiting Lecturer in Piano Pedagogy at the University of Illinois at Urbana-Champaign. Ms. Linn holds a B.M. and M.M. in Piano Performance from the University of Missouri-Kansas City (UMKC) Conservatory of Music.

Mike Springer

MIKE SPRINGER maintains an active schedule as a teacher, composer/arranger, pianist and adjudicator in the Dallas, Texas area. Mr. Springer has composed and arranged extensively for piano, electronic media (MIDI), vocal ensemble, and wind ensemble. Mr. Springer is an accomplished performer in classical and jazz idioms. He has been the pianist at Cornerstone United Methodist Church in Garland, Texas for over twelve years. Mr. Springer studied with Dr. Pamela Paul at the University of North Texas, where he earned his Bachelor of Music and Master of Music degrees in Piano Performance.

Christos Tsitsaros

CHRISTOS TSITSAROS is currently Assistant Professor of Piano Pedagogy at the University of Illinois at Urbana-Champaign. The recipient of numerous scholarships and awards, Dr. Tsitsaros has appeared in recitals, chamber music concerts and as soloist in Europe and the United States. Dr. Tsitsaros holds the Diplôme Supérieur d'Execution from the École Normale de Musique de Paris, an Artist Diploma and M.M. degree from Indiana University, and a D.M.A. (piano performance) from the University of Illinois. A recent CD recording of his piano compositions is available through Centaur Records, Inc.

Showcase Solos

Showcase Solos is a graded series of solo and duet sheet music for piano, including original compositions, seasonal music, and arrangements of folk and popular melodies for piano. Ranging from Early Elementary through Late Intermediate repertoire, these imaginative pieces provide excellent supplementary material for any method, and are a perfect complement to the **Hal Leonard Student Piano Library**.

Excellent Material for:
- Recitals
- Special Rewards
- Student Incentives
- Seasonal Enjoyment

OVER **60** GREAT SOLOS!

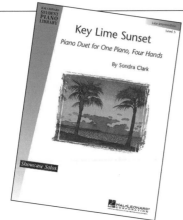

Pre-Staff (Early Level 1)
00296367   Bumper Cars *(Jennifer Linn)*
00296368   The Hungry Spider *(Jennifer Linn)*

Early Elementary (Level 1)
00296127   Japanese Garden *(Jennifer Linn)*
00296128   Jazz Jig *(Phillip Keveren)*
00296169   Ocean Breezes *(Mona Rejino)*
00296154   Sledding Fun *(Peggy Otwell)*

Elementary (Level 2)
00296315   Accidental Wizard *(Phillip Keveren)*
00296312   Gone Fishin' – 1P, 4H Duet *(Carol Klose)*
00296151   Joyful Bells *(Jennifer Linn)*
00296129   Lost Treasure *(Mona Rejino)*
00296313   Party Cat Parade *(Jennifer Linn)*
00296314   Rainy Day Play *(Carol Klose)*
00296170   Veggie Song *(Jennifer Linn)*

Late Elementary (Level 3)
00296131   Caravan *(Carol Klose)*
00296369   Copycat! – 1P, 4H Duet *(Deborah Brady)*
00296130   The Happy Walrus *(Mike Springer)*
00296152   Harvest Dance *(Jennifer Linn)*
00296133   Hummingbird *(Jennifer Linn)*
00296172   Little Bird *(Carol Klose)*
00296171   Quick Spin In A Fast Car *(Phillip Keveren)*
00296132   Soft Shoe Shuffle *(Bill Boyd)*
00296148   White Christmas *(Berlin/arr. Mona Rejino)*

Early Intermediate (Level 4)
00296150   Autumn Sunset *(Mike Springer)*
00296139   Castilian Dreamer *(Carol Klose)*
00296317   Cheshire Cat Cool *(Rosemary Barrett Byers)*
00296135   Jump Around Rag *(Bill Boyd)*
00296141   Little Mazurka *(Christos Tsitsaros)*
00296173   Meaghan's Melody *(Jennifer Linn)*
00296371   Mountain Splendor *(Mona Rejino)*
00296137   Peaceful Tide *(Phillip Keveren)*
00296140   Prelude To Rain *(Mike Springer)*
00296370   Reflections In The Moonlight *(Mike Springer)*
00296316   Seaside Stride *(Mike Springer)*
00296143   Smilin' Mr. Dile *(Rosemary Barrett Byers)*
00296174   Snap To It! *(Mona Rejino)*

Intermediate (Level 5)
00296318   Café Waltz *(Matthew Edwards)*
00296136   Forever In My Heart *(Phillip Keveren)*
00296138   Gypsy Dance *(Christos Tsitsaros)*
00296144   Indigo Bay *(Jennifer Linn)*
00296175   Jesters *(Christos Tsitsaros)*
00296311   Key Lime Sunset – 1P, 4H Duet *(Sondra Clark)*
00296366   Miami Mambo – 1P, 4H Duet *(Sondra Clark)*
00296142   Salsa Picante *(Carol Klose)*
00296372   Sarasota Circus – 1P, 4H Duet *(Sondra Clark)*
00296134   Sassy Samba *(Mona Rejino)*
00296153   Skater's Dream *(Carol Klose)*
00296176   Twilight On The Lake *(Matthew Edwards)*
00296145   White Christmas *(Berlin/arr. Phillip Keveren)*
00296149   Witch On The Wind *(Rosemary Barrett Byers)*

Visit our website
www.halleonard.com
for the newest titles in this series.

Composer Showcase

This series showcases the varied talents of our **Hal Leonard Student Piano Library** family of composers. Here is where you will find great original piano music by your favorite composers, including Phillip Keveren, Carol Klose, Jennifer Linn, Bill Boyd, Bruce Berr, and many others. Carefully graded and leveled for easy selection, each book contains gems that are certain to become tomorrow's classics!

Elementary

00290425	Jazz Starters *(Bill Boyd)*

Late Elementary

00296354	Coral Reef Suite *(Carol Klose)*
00290359	Imaginations In Style *(Bruce Berr)*
00290434	Jazz Starters II *(Bill Boyd)*
00290465	Jazz Starters III *(Bill Boyd)*
00296361	Mouse On A Mirror & Other Contemporary Character Pieces *(Phillip Keveren)*
00296374	Shifty-Eyed Blues & More Contemporary Character Pieces *(Phillip Keveren)*
00296353	Tex-Mex Rex *(Phillip Keveren)*

Early Intermediate

00290360	Explorations In Style *(Bruce Berr)*
00296373	Monday's Child *(Deborah Brady)*
00290417	Think Jazz! *(Bill Boyd)*

Intermediate

00296356	Concerto For Young Pianists – 2P, 4H *(Matthew Edwards)*
00240435	Jazz Delights *(Bill Boyd)*
00296355	Les Petites Impressions *(Jennifer Linn)*

Visit our website **www.halleonard.com** for full descriptions and song lists for each of the books listed here, and to view the newest titles in this series.

The Phillip Keveren Series

African-American Spirituals
20 popular spirituals, including: Deep River • Every Time I Feel the Spirit • Go Down, Moses • Swing Low, Sweet Chariot • and more.
00310610   Easy Piano (Level 4/5)

The Beatles
18 Fab Four favorites: And I Love Her • Hey Jude • In My Life • Let It Be • Norwegian Wood • Penny Lane • Yesterday • and more.
00306412   Piano Solo (Late Intermediate/Advanced)

Broadway's Best
16 Broadway standards: All I Ask of You • Cabaret • Edelweiss • Some Enchanted Evening • and more.
00310669   Piano Solo (Late Intermediate/Advanced)

A Celtic Christmas
16 Christmas carols: God Rest Ye Merry, Gentlemen • Here We Come A-Wassailing • The Holly and the Ivy • Irish Carol • Lo, How a Rose E'er Blooming • Wexford Carol • and more.
00310629   Piano Solo (Late Intermediate/Advanced)

The Celtic Collection
15 traditional Irish folk tunes: Be Thou My Vision • Danny Boy (Londonderry Air) • Molly Malone (Cockles & Mussels) • 'Tis the Last Rose of Summer • The Wearing of the Green • and more.
00310549   Piano Solo (Late Intermediate/Advanced)

Children's Favorite Movie Songs
15 favorites from films: Beauty and the Beast • Can You Feel the Love Tonight • So Long, Farewell • Tomorrow • and more.
00310838   Big-Note Piano (Level 3)

Christian Children's Favorites
25 songs: The B-I-B-L-E • Deep and Wide • Down in My Heart • Jesus Loves Me • This Little Light of Mine • and more.
00310837   Beginning Piano Solos (Level 2-3)

Cinema Classics
15 movie themes: Endless Love • My Heart Will Go On • Raiders March • The Rainbow Connection • Romeo and Juliet (Love Theme) • Tears in Heaven • and more.
00310607   Piano Solos (Late Intermediate/Advanced)

A Classical Christmas
20 beloved carols: Angels We Have Heard on High • Away in a Manger • Joy to the World • O Holy Night • Still, Still, Still • We Three Kings of Orient Are • and more.
00310769   Easy Piano (Level 4/5)

Contemporary Hits
16 songs: Amazed • Angel • Breathe • I Hope You Dance • Only Time • There You'll Be • When You Say Nothing at All • and more.
00310907   Big-Note Piano (Level 3)

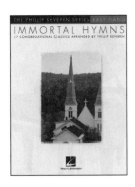

Gospel Treasures
18 beautiful arrangements: Amazing Grace • His Eye Is on the Sparrow • Just a Closer Walk with Thee • Shall We Gather at the River? • and more.
00310805   Easy Piano (Level 4/5)

I Could Sing Of Your Love Forever
15 songs of praise: Awesome God • I Could Sing of Your Love Forever • I Love You Lord • The Potter's Hand • and more.
00310905   Piano Solo (Late Intermediate/Advanced)

Immortal Hymns
17 everlasting favorites: All Hail the Power of Jesus' Name • Holy, Holy, Holy • In the Garden • Just As I Am • and more.
00310798   Easy Piano (Level 4/5)

Jingle Jazz
17 Christmas standards arranged with a touch of cool: The Christmas Song (Chestnuts Roasting on an Open Fire) • I'll Be Home for Christmas • Merry Christmas, Darling • and more.
00310762   Piano Solo (Late Intermediate/Advanced)

Joy To The World
18 carols: Angels We have Heard on High • Deck the Halls • The Friendly Beasts • O Holy Night • Silent Night • What Child Is This? • and more.
00310888   Big-Note Piano (Level 3)

Kids' Favorites
25 songs: Alouette • Eensy Weensy Spider • London Bridge • Pop Goes the Weasel • Twinkle, Twinkle Little Star • Yankee Doodle • and more.
00310822   Beginning Piano Solos (Level 2-3)

Let Freedom Ring!
15 favorites: America, the Beautiful • My Country, 'Tis of Thee • Stars and Stripes Forever • and more.
00310839   Piano Solo (Late Intermediate/Advanced)

Love Songs
17 romantic favorites: Can't Help Falling in Love • I'll Never Love This Way Again • Love Story • Save the Best for Last • We've Only Just Begun • A Whole New World • You Are So Beautiful • and more.
00310744   Easy Piano (Level 4/5)

Pop Ballads
17 pop classics: Angel • The First Time Ever I Saw Your Face • From a Distance • Lady in Red • My Heart Will Go On • Nadia's Theme • Rainy Days and Mondays • The Way We Were • and more.
00220036   Easy Piano (Level 4/5)

Richard Rodgers Piano Solos
17 classics: Edelweiss • My Funny Valentine • Some Enchanted Evening • You'll Never Walk Alone • and more.
00310755   Piano Solos (Late Intermediate/Advanced)

Shout To The Lord
14 favorite praise songs: As the Deer • El Shaddai • Oh Lord, You're Beautiful • Shine, Jesus, Shine • Shout to the Lord • and more.
00310699   Piano Solo (Late Intermediate/Advanced)

Sweet Land Of Liberty
15 patriotic favorites: America, the Beautiful • Hail to the Chief • The Star Spangled Banner • Stars and Striped Forever • and more.
00310840   Easy Piano (Level 4/5)

The Nutcracker
8 Favorites from Tchaikovsky's holiday classic: Overture • March • Dance of the Sugar Plum Fairy • Russian Dance • Arabian Dance • and more.
00310908   Big-Note Piano (Level 3)

This Is Your Time
15 songs: Can't Live a Day • Every Season • Go in Sin No More • Jesus Will Still Be There • Lamb of God • Shine On Us • This Is Your Time • and more.
00310956   Big-Note Piano (Level 3)

Timeless Praise
20 sacred classics: How Beautiful • How Majestic Is Your Name • Lord, I Lift Your Name on High • People Need the Lord • There Is a Redeemer • Thy Word • and more.
00310712   Easy Piano (Level 4/5)

21 Great Classics
21 beloved classical masterworks: Air on the G String • Canon in D Major • Eine Kleine Nachtmusik • Hallelujah! • Jesu, Joy of Man's Desiring • and more.
00310717   Easy Piano (Level 4/5)

Notespellers, Assignment Books, Flash Cards and Other Teaching Aids

BOOK 1
Along the Music Trail with Spike and Party Cat
Activities that help students use the musical alphabet to read and write notes on the staff.
00296088

BOOK 2
A Visit to Piano Park with Spike and Party Cat
Assignments that help students use the musical alphabet to read and write notes on the staff, identify intervals, and write sharps and flats.
00296089

BOOK 3
A Visit to Music City with Spike and Party Cat
Assignments that help students sharpen their music reading skills, learn to read ledger-line notes, and identify intervals, half and whole steps, and major/minor five-finger patterns.
00296167

Pocket Music Dictionary
The most contemporary music dictionary on the market! Conveniently divided into three main sections: The Dictionary of Music Terms contains definitions for over 2,000 musical terms; The Dictionary of Musicians provides more than 400 brief biographies of composers & musicians; a collection of Reference Charts gives instant, at-a-glance summaries of the essentials of music.
00183006

Flash Cards
Set A
120 color-coded cards to review basic musical symbols, all notes from low ledger C to high ledger C, and rhythm patterns in 4/4 and 3/4.
00296034

Set B
120 color-coded cards to review musical terms, scales, key signatures, and chord progressions in C, Am, G, Em, F, Dm, and rhythm patterns in 2/4, 3/4, 4/4, 3/8, and 6/8.
00296035

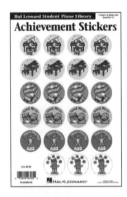

Achievement Stickers
Featuring our loveable method mascots Spike and Party Cat, plus other eye-catching illustrations from our piano method books. Includes 8 stickers each of 6 different designs – 48 one-inch full color stickers in all.
00296185

My Music Journal
Includes a one-year practice planner with lesson assignments, a dictionary of musical terms, a music history timeline, a keyboard guide, and staff paper.
00296040

My Practice Record
Includes 32 weeks of lesson assignments and a music dictionary.
00296046

Music Manuscript Paper
32-page, wide-staff manuscript paper, in an 8½" x 8½" booklet. Includes a comprehensive music notation guide & glossary of terms for student reference.
00296307

Hal Leonard Student Keyboard Guide
Handy reference for beginning students. The front of the guide fits behind all 88 keys of any piano, and the back of the guide is a practice keyboard.
00296039

HLSPL Method Books

BOOK 1

Title	Item No.	Price
Teacher's Guide & Planning Chart	00296048	$ 6.95
Piano Lessons Book/CD	00296177	7.95
Piano Lessons	00296001	5.95
Piano Lessons CD	00296004	5.95
Piano Lessons GM Disk	00296005	9.95
Piano Practice Games	00296002	5.95
Piano Technique	00296105	5.95
Piano Technique CD	00296112	5.95
Piano Technique GM Disk	00296113	9.95
Piano Solos	00296003	5.95
Piano Solos CD	00296017	5.95
Piano Solos GM Disk	00296018	9.95
Piano Theory Workbook	00296023	5.95
Notespeller For Piano	00296088	5.95

BOOK 2

Title	Item No.	Price
Teacher's Guide & Planning Chart	00296362	$ 6.95
Piano Lessons Book/CD	00296178	7.95
Piano Lessons	00296006	5.95
Piano Lessons CD	00296009	5.95
Piano Lessons GM Disk	00296010	9.95
Piano Practice Games	00296007	5.95
Piano Technique	00296106	5.95
Piano Technique CD	00296117	5.95
Piano Technique GM Disk	00296118	9.95
Piano Solos	00296008	5.95
Piano Solos CD	00296019	5.95
Piano Solos GM Disk	00296020	9.95
Piano Theory Workbook	00296024	5.95
Notespeller For Piano	00296089	5.95

BOOK 3

Title	Item No.	Price
Piano Lessons Book/CD	00296179	$ 7.95
Piano Lessons	00296011	5.95
Piano Lessons CD	00296014	5.95
Piano Lessons GM Disk	00296015	9.95
Piano Practice Games	00296012	5.95
Piano Technique	00296114	5.95
Piano Technique CD	00296119	5.95
Piano Technique GM Disk	00296120	9.95
Piano Solos	00296013	5.95
Piano Solos CD	00296021	5.95
Piano Solos GM Disk	00296022	9.95
Piano Theory Workbook	00296025	5.95
Notespeller For Piano	00296167	5.95

BOOK 4

Title	Item No.	Price
Piano Lessons Book/CD	00296180	$ 7.95
Piano Lessons	00296026	5.95
Piano Lessons CD	00296029	5.95
Piano Lessons GM Disk	00296030	9.95
Piano Practice Games	00296027	5.95
Piano Technique	00296115	5.95
Piano Technique CD	00296121	5.95
Piano Technique GM Disk	00296122	9.95
Piano Solos	00296028	5.95
Piano Solos CD	00296036	5.95
Piano Solos GM Disk	00296037	9.95
Piano Theory Workbook	00296038	5.95

BOOK 5

Title	Item No.	Price
Piano Lessons Book/CD	00296181	$ 7.95
Piano Lessons	00296041	6.95
Piano Lessons CD	00296044	5.95
Piano Lessons GM Disk	00296045	9.95
Piano Technique	00296116	5.95
Piano Technique CD	00296123	5.95
Piano Technique GM Disk	00296124	9.95
Piano Solos	00296043	5.95
Piano Solos CD	00296071	5.95
Piano Solos GM Disk	00296072	9.95
Piano Theory Workbook	00296042	5.95

Supplementary Books

TECHNIQUE CLASSICS

Title	Item No.	Price
Czerny – Selections From The Little Pianist, Opus 823 Book	00296364	$ 5.95
Czerny – Selections From The Little Pianist, Opus 823 Book/CD	00296363	9.95
Czerny – Selections From The Little Pianist, Opus 823 GM Disk	00296365	9.95
Hanon For The Developing Pianist Book	00296183	5.95
Hanon For The Developing Pianist Book/CD	00296165	9.95
Hanon For The Developing Pianist GM Disk	00296184	9.95

CHRISTMAS PIANO SOLOS

Title	Item No.	Price
Christmas Piano Solos Level 1	00296049	$ 5.95
Christmas Piano Solos Level 1 CD	00296081	10.95
Christmas Piano Solos Level 1 GM Disk	00296101	12.95
Christmas Piano Solos Level 2	00296050	5.95
Christmas Piano Solos Level 2 CD	00296082	10.95
Christmas Piano Solos Level 2 GM Disk	00296102	12.95
Christmas Piano Solos Level 3	00296051	5.95
Christmas Piano Solos Level 3 CD	00296083	10.95
Christmas Piano Solos Level 3 GM Disk	00296103	12.95
Christmas Piano Solos Level 4	00296052	5.95
Christmas Piano Solos Level 4 CD	00296084	10.95
Christmas Piano Solos Level 4 GM Disk	00296104	12.95
Christmas Piano Solos Level 5	00296146	6.95
Christmas Piano Solos Level 5 CD	00296159	10.95
Christmas Piano Solos Level 5 GM Disk	00296162	12.95

All prices listed in US funds. Prices, contents, and availability subject to change without notice.

Title	Item No.	Price
SEASONAL JEWISH SONGBOOKS		
Festive Chanukah Songs Level 2	00296194	$ 5.95
Festive Songs For The Jewish Holidays Level 3	00296195	6.95
POPULAR PIANO SOLOS		
Popular Piano Solos Level 1	00296031	$ 5.95
Popular Piano Solos Level 1 CD	00296093	10.95
Popular Piano Solos Level 1 GM Disk	00296094	12.95
Popular Piano Solos Level 2	00296032	5.95
Popular Piano Solos Level 2 CD	00296095	10.95
Popular Piano Solos Level 2 GM Disk	00296096	12.95
Popular Piano Solos Level 3	00296033	5.95
Popular Piano Solos Level 3 CD	00296097	10.95
Popular Piano Solos Level 3 GM Disk	00296098	12.95
Popular Piano Solos Level 4	00296053	5.95
Popular Piano Solos Level 4 CD	00296099	10.95
Popular Piano Solos Level 4 GM Disk	00296100	12.95
Popular Piano Solos Level 5	00296147	6.95
Popular Piano Solos Level 5 CD	00296157	10.95
Popular Piano Solos Level 5 GM Disk	00296158	12.95
More Popular Piano Solos Level 1	00296189	5.95
More Popular Piano Solos Level 1 CD	00296260	10.95
More Popular Piano Solos Level 1 GM Disk	00296263	12.95
More Popular Piano Solos Level 2	00296190	5.95
More Popular Piano Solos Level 2 CD	00296261	10.95
More Popular Piano Solos Level 2 GM Disk	00296264	12.95
More Popular Piano Solos Level 3	00296191	6.95
More Popular Piano Solos Level 3 CD	00296262	10.95
More Popular Piano Solos Level 3 GM Disk	00296265	12.95
More Popular Piano Solos Level 4	00296192	6.95
More Popular Piano Solos Level 4 CD	00296274	10.95
More Popular Piano Solos Level 4 GM Disk	00296276	12.95
More Popular Piano Solos Level 5	00296193	6.95
More Popular Piano Solos Level 5 CD	00296275	10.95
More Popular Piano Solos Level 5 GM Disk	00296277	12.95
PATRIOTIC SONGBOOKS		
God Bless America® Patriotic Piano Solos Level 1	00296249	$ 5.95
God Bless America Patriotic Piano Solos Level 2	00296250	5.95
God Bless America Patriotic Piano Solos Level 3	00296255	5.95
God Bless America Patriotic Piano Duets Level 3	00296251	5.95
God Bless America Patriotic Piano Solos Level 4	00296256	5.95
God Bless America Patriotic Piano Duets Level 4	00296252	5.95
God Bless America Patriotic Piano Solos Level 5	00296257	6.95
God Bless America Patriotic Piano Duets Level 5	00296253	5.95

Visit Hal Leonard Online at
www.halleonard.com
or e-mail us at
piano@halleonard.com

Title	Item No.	Price
TRADITIONAL HYMNS		
Traditional Hymns Level 1	00296196	$ 5.95
Traditional Hymns Level 1 CD	00296278	10.95
Traditional Hymns Level 1 GM Disk	00296283	12.95
Traditional Hymns Level 2	00296198	5.95
Traditional Hymns Level 2 CD	00296279	10.95
Traditional Hymns Level 2 GM Disk	00296284	12.95
Traditional Hymns Level 3	00296197	6.95
Traditional Hymns Level 3 CD	00296280	10.95
Traditional Hymns Level 3 GM Disk	00296285	12.95
Traditional Hymns Level 4	00296199	6.95
Traditional Hymns Level 4 CD	00296281	10.95
Traditional Hymns Level 4 GM Disk	00296286	12.95
Traditional Hymns Level 5	00296200	6.95
Traditional Hymns Level 5 CD	00296282	10.95
Traditional Hymns Level 5 GM Disk	00296287	12.95
CLASSICAL THEMES		
Classical Themes Level 1	00296323	$ 5.95
Classical Themes Level 1 CD	00296328	10.95
Classical Themes Level 1 GM Disk	00296333	12.95
Classical Themes Level 2	00296324	5.95
Classical Themes Level 2 CD	00296329	10.95
Classical Themes Level 2 GM Disk	00296334	12.95
Classical Themes Level 3	00296325	5.95
Classical Themes Level 3 CD	00296330	10.95
Classical Themes Level 3 GM Disk	00296335	12.95
Classical Themes Level 4	00296326	5.95
Classical Themes Level 4 CD	00296331	10.95
Classical Themes Level 4 GM Disk	00296336	12.95
Classical Themes Level 5	00296327	6.95
Classical Themes Level 5 CD	00296332	10.95
Classical Themes Level 5 GM Disk	00296337	12.95

COMPOSER SHOWCASE

ELEMENTARY (HLSPL LEVEL 2)		
Jazz Starters/*Bill Boyd*	00290425	$ 6.95

LATE ELEMENTARY (HLSPL LEVEL 3)		
Coral Reef Suite/*Carol Klose*	00296354	$ 5.95
Imaginations In Style/*Bruce Berr*	00290359	5.95
Jazz Starters II/*Bill Boyd*	00290434	6.95
Jazz Starters III/*Bill Boyd*	00290465	6.95
Mouse On A Mirror & Other Contemporary Character Pieces/*Phillip Keveren*	00296361	6.95
Shifty-Eyed Blues & More Contemporary Character Pieces/*Phillip Keveren*	00296374	6.95
Tex-Mex Rex/*Phillip Keveren*	00296353	5.95

EARLY INTERMEDIATE (HLSPL LEVEL 4)		
Explorations In Style/*Bruce Berr*	00290360	$ 6.95
Monday's Child/*Deborah Brady*	00296373	6.95
Think Jazz!/*Bill Boyd*	00290417	9.95

INTERMEDIATE (HLSPL LEVEL 5)		
Concerto For Young Pianists (2P, 4H)/*Matthew Edwards*	00296356	$11.95
Jazz Delights/*Bill Boyd*	00240435	6.95
Les Petites Impressions/*Jennifer Linn*	00296355	6.95

All prices listed in US funds. Prices, contents, and availability subject to change without notice.

SHOWCASE SOLOS

Title	Item No.	Price
PRE-STAFF (HLSPL EARLY LEVEL 1)		
Bumper Cars/*Jennifer Linn*	00296367	$ 2.50
The Hungry Spider/*Jennifer Linn*	00296368	2.50
EARLY ELEMENTARY (HLSPL LEVEL 1)		
"C" Is For Cookie/*arr. Phillip Keveren*	00296267	$ 3.95
God Bless America®/Berlin/*arr. Mona Rejino*	00296238	2.95
Japanese Garden/*Jennifer Linn*	00296127	2.50
Jazz Jig/*Phillip Keveren*	00296128	2.50
My Country, 'Tis Of Thee (America)/*arr. Carol Klose*	00296243	2.50
Ocean Breezes/*Mona Rejino*	00296169	2.50
Sledding Fun/*Peggy Otwell*	00296154	2.50
Winnie The Pooh/*arr. Fred Kern*	00296266	3.95
ELEMENTARY (HLSPL LEVEL 2)		
Accidental Wizard/*Phillip Keveren*	00296315	$ 2.50
America, The Beautiful/*Mona Rejino*	00296244	2.50
God Bless America/Berlin/*arr. Carol Klose*	00296239	2.95
Gone Fishin' (1P, 4H Duet)/*Carol Klose*	00296312	2.50
Joyful Bells/*Jennifer Linn*	00296151	2.50
Lost Treasure/*Mona Rejino*	00296129	2.50
Party Cat Parade/*Jennifer Linn*	00296313	2.50
Veggie Song/*Jennifer Linn*	00296170	2.50
Rainy Day Play/*Carol Klose*	00296314	2.50
Sing/*Fred Kern*	00296268	3.95
LATE ELEMENTARY (HLSPL LEVEL 3)		
Caravan/*Carol Klose*	00296131	$ 2.50
Copycat! (1P, 4H Duet)/*Deborah Brady*	00296369	2.50
God Bless America/Berlin/*arr. Jennifer Linn*	00296240	3.95
The Happy Walrus/*Mike Springer*	00296130	2.50
Harvest Dance/*Jennifer Linn*	00296152	2.50
Hummingbird/*Jennifer Linn*	00296133	2.50
Little Bird/*Carol Klose*	00296172	2.50
Quick Spin In A Fast Car/*Phillip Keveren*	00296171	2.50
Raiders March/*Phillip Keveren*	00296269	3.95
Soft Shoe Shuffle/*Bill Boyd*	00296132	2.50
A Star-Spangled Salute/*Jennifer Linn*	00296245	2.95
This Is A Great Country/Berlin/*arr. Barrett Byers*	00296254	3.95
White Christmas/Berlin/*arr. Mona Rejino*	00296148	3.95
EARLY INTERMEDIATE (HLSPL LEVEL 4)		
Autumn Sunset/*Mike Springer*	00296150	$ 2.50
Castilian Dreamer/*Carol Klose*	00296139	2.50
Cheshire Cat Cool/*Rosemary Barrett Byers*	00296317	2.50
Cruella de Vil/*arr. Mona Rejino*	00296270	3.95
God Bless America/Berlin/*arr. Fred Kern*	00296241	3.95
Jump Around Rag/*Bill Boyd*	00296135	2.50

Title	Item No.	Price
EARLY INTERMEDIATE (HLSPL LEVEL 4) Con't		
Little Mazurka/*Christos Tsitsaros*	00296141	$ 2.50
Meaghan's Melody/*Jennifer Linn*	00296173	2.95
Mountain Splendor/*Mona Rejino*	00296371	2.50
Peaceful Tide/*Phillip Keveren*	00296137	2.95
Prelude To Rain/*Mike Springer*	00296140	2.95
Reflections In The Moonlight/*Mike Springer*	00296370	2.50
Seaside Stride/*Mike Springer*	00296316	2.50
Smilin' Mr. Dile/*Rosemary Barrett Byers*	00296143	2.50
Snap To It!/*Mona Rejino*	00296174	2.50
A Spoonful Of Sugar/*Mona Rejino*	00296271	3.95
This Is My Country/*Matthew Edwards*	00296246	3.95
INTERMEDIATE (HLSPL LEVEL 5)		
America, The Beautiful/*Christos Tsitsaros*	00296248	$ 2.95
Café Waltz/*Matthew Edwards*	00296318	2.95
Battle Hymn Of The Republic/*Fred Kern*	00296247	2.95
Forever In My Heart/*Phillip Keveren*	00296136	2.95
God Bless America/Berlin/ *arr. Phillip Keveren*	00296242	3.95
Gypsy Dance/*Christos Tsitsaros*	00296138	2.50
Indigo Bay/*Jennifer Linn*	00296144	2.95
Jesters/*Christos Tsitsaros*	00296175	2.50
Key Lime Sunset (1P, 4H)/*Sondra Clark*	00296311	3.95
Miami Mambo (1P, 4H Duet)/*Sondra Clark*	00296366	3.95
Mission: Impossible Theme/*Fred Kern*	00296272	3.95
Salsa Picante/*Carol Klose*	00296142	2.95
Sarasota Circus (1P, 4H Duet)/*Sondra Clark*	00296372	3.95
Sassy Samba/*Mona Rejino*	00296134	2.95
Skater's Dream/*Carol Klose*	00296153	2.95
Twilight On The Lake/*Matthew Edwards*	00296176	2.95
White Christmas/Berlin/*arr. Phillip Keveren*	00296145	3.95
Witch On The Wind/*Rosemary Barrett Byers*	00296149	2.50
Y.M.C.A./*Fred Kern*	00296273	3.95

PIANO ENSEMBLES

Title	Item No.	Price
Piano Ensembles Level 1	00296064	$ 5.95
Piano Ensembles Level 1 CD	00296073	5.95
Piano Ensembles Level 1 GM Disk	00296074	9.95
Piano Ensembles Level 2	00296065	5.95
Piano Ensembles Level 2 CD	00296075	5.95
Piano Ensembles Level 2 GM Disk	00296076	9.95
Piano Ensembles Level 3	00296066	5.95
Piano Ensembles Level 3 CD	00296077	5.95
Piano Ensembles Level 3 GM Disk	00296078	9.95
Piano Ensembles Level 4	00296067	5.95
Piano Ensembles Level 4 CD	00296079	5.95
Piano Ensembles Level 4 GM Disk	00296080	9.95
Piano Ensembles Level 5	00296090	5.95
Piano Ensembles Level 5 CD	00296091	5.95
Piano Ensembles Level 5 GM Disk	00296092	9.95

All prices listed in US funds. Prices, contents, and availability subject to change without notice.

Title	Item No.	Price
THE PHILLIP KEVEREN SERIES		
BEGINNING PIANO SOLOS (ELEMENTARY HLSPL LEVEL 2-3)		
Christian Children's Favorites	00310837	$ 9.95
Kids' Favorites	00310822	9.95
BIG-NOTE PIANO (LATE ELEMENTARY HLSPL LEVEL 3)		
Children's Favorite Movie Songs	00310838	$ 10.95
Contemporary Hits	00310907	12.95
Joy To The World	00310888	10.95
The Nutcracker	00310908	8.95
This Is Your Time	00310956	10.95
EASY PIANO (EARLY INTERMEDIATE HLSPL LEVEL 4/5)		
African-American Spirituals	00310610	$ 9.95
A Classical Christmas	00310769	10.95
Gospel Treasures	00310805	10.95
Immortal Hymns	00310798	10.95
Love Songs	00310744	10.95
Pop Ballads	00220036	12.95
Sweet Land Of Liberty	00310840	9.95
Timeless Praise	00310712	12.95
21 Great Classics	00310717	10.95
PIANO SOLO (LATE INTERMEDIATE/ADVANCED)		
The Beatles	00306412	$ 12.95
Broadway's Best	00310669	12.95
A Celtic Christmas	00310629	10.95
The Celtic Collection	00310549	12.95
Cinema Classics	00310607	12.95
I Could Sing Of Your Love Forever	00310905	12.95
Jingle Jazz	00310762	12.95
Let Freedom Ring!	00310839	9.95
Richard Rodgers Piano Solos	00310755	12.95
Shout To The Lord	00310699	10.95
TEACHING MATERIALS		
Music Flash Cards – Set A	00296034	$ 3.95
Music Flash Cards – Set B	00296035	3.95
Achievement Stickers	00296185	2.50
Music Manuscript Paper	00296307	1.95
My Music Journal	00296040	3.95
My Practice Record	00296046	.75
Student Keyboard Guide	00296039	1.95
Pocket Music Dictionary	00183006	4.95

HLSPL French Language Editions

Title	Item No.	Price
BOOK 1		
Piano Lessons	00296202	$ 5.95
Piano Lessons CD	00296207	5.95
Piano Solos	00296212	5.95
Piano Solos CD	00296217	5.95
BOOK 2		
Piano Lessons	00296203	$ 5.95
Piano Lessons CD	00296208	5.95
Piano Solos	00296213	5.95
Piano Solos CD	00296218	5.95
BOOK 3		
Piano Lessons	00296204	$ 5.95
Piano Lessons CD	00296209	5.95
Piano Solos	00296214	5.95
Piano Solos CD	00296219	5.95
BOOK 4		
Piano Lessons	00296205	$ 5.95
Piano Lessons CD	00296210	5.95
Piano Solos	00296215	5.95
Piano Solos CD	00296220	5.95
BOOK 5		
Piano Lessons	00296206	$ 5.95
Piano Lessons CD	00296211	5.95
Piano Solos	00296216	5.95
Piano Solos CD	00296221	5.95

Visit your favorite music dealer to place your order.

HAL•LEONARD®

To find a music dealer near you,
visit **www.halleonard.com**

All prices listed in US funds. Prices, contents, and availability subject to change without notice.

Are we in touch with you?

Send us your name and address and
we'll send you our **FREE** teacher newsletter, *In Touch!*

Hal Leonard Corporation • Attn: Heidi Steeno
7777 W. Bluemound Road • P.O. Box 13819
Milwaukee, Wisconsin 53213

or e-mail us at **piano@halleonard.com**